D1478558

YOUR TIME IS AT HAND

The New Age Study of Humanity's Purpose, Inc.
P.O. Box 41883
Tucson, Arizona 85717

New Age Study of Humanity's Purpose, Inc.
P.O. Box 41883
Tucson, AZ 85717

Cover and Illustrations by Sharon Maia Nichols

Manufactured in the United States of America

Library of Congress Cataloging in Publication Data
ISBN 09615287-2-9
TX 3 298 501

First Edition January 11, 1992
Second Edition June 21, 1993

For information on Visionary Art by Sharon Maia Nichols, contact
The New Age Study of Humanity's Purpose
PO Box 41883
Tucson, AZ 85717

DEDICATED TO
THE ASCENSION OF
PLANET EARTH

ACKNOWLEDGMENTS

I acknowledge, with abounding joy, the awakening Divinity in every heart.

I also send my deepest love and gratitude to:

My wonderful family–my husband, Dickie, who has been the love of my life since I was thirteen; my son Joao and my daughter Victoria who both make me laugh and greatly add to the Light of my life; my two beautiful grandsons, Dylan and Hayden, who have come to teach me about God; and the rest of my extended family, who encourage and lovingly support me.

I give my eternal gratitude to my dear friend and co-worker Kay E. Meyer, who diligently keeps the logistical mechanism of our Spiritual work on course.

I give my deepest love to all of the Lightworkers who serve with me selflessly and joyfully.

And, I give thanks to our Father-Mother God for allowing me the sacred privilege of walking this sweet Earth during her time of rebirth and transformation.

TABLE OF CONTENTS

CHAPTER ONE

WHAT DOES THE
NEW AGE REALLY MEAN?

These are very challenging times, but they are also marvelously wonderful times. All we have to do is turn on the news or read a newspaper to realize things are happening on this Planet at an incredibly rapid pace. Sometimes the things occurring seem mind boggling and overwhelming. Other times they seem like the natural order of change. We are in the midst of what is known as a "Cosmic Moment," and whether we are consciously aware of it or not, this is the moment we have all been preparing for for aeons of time. This is the moment when this sweet Earth and all life evolving upon her are destined to move through the doorway into Octaves of Perfection to continue the evolutionary journey back to the Heart of our Father-Mother God. Much preparation has been made for this vibrational shift, and even though much work is still necessary, our victory is assured.

Many wonderous things have occurred over the past few years to prepare us for this quantum leap into the frequencies of Fourth Dimensional Perfection. If you are hearing of this transformational process for the first time, it may sound a little bit like science fiction, but in actuality, this information is recorded clearly in the Akashic Records of this sacred Planet and will one day be readily accepted as history.

This is the dawn of what is being heralded as the Permanent Golden Age, the initial impulse of the New Age of Enlightenment. It is the moment on Earth when we will correct our course, reclaim the vision and return to the Divine Plan in which the Cosmic Fiat of "As above, so below" will be the order of the "New Day." Heaven shall indeed manifest on Earth, and the decree of "Thy Kingdom come, Thy Will be done on Earth as It is in Heaven" will be fulfilled.

As is always the case, when new levels of wisdom and understanding begin filtering into the consciousness of Humanity, it initially causes confusion and often even fear. Our existing belief systems are challenged, and we feel threatened and vulnerable. We each try to interpret what is happening through the eyes of our personal experience which creates even more confusion because no two people have experienced life in exactly the same way. This results in myriad scenarios about what is real and true. In order for us to dissipate our fear and increase our feelings of security, we talk ourselves into believing that what we perceive to be true is "right," and therefore anything else must be "wrong." This creates a comfort zone that is tolerable for us and allows us to feel safe. The problem is, of course, that this also creates separation, and it closes our minds, preventing us from being able to receive greater levels of understanding from the Realms of Truth.

This phenomenom is occurring now on Earth. Many religious leaders are vehemently resisting the wisdom that is pouring into the consciousness of Humanity. Because the new information exposes our misinformation and our disinformation in the Light of Truth, it is normal for people to feverishly read the Holy Books and try to reassure themselves by literally interpreting the message to fit their distorted belief systems. Unfortunately, this only increases the fear and deepens the chasm of ignorance and separation.

There is so much confusion and so much fear about what is happening on Earth now that some religious leaders are professing the New Age of Enlightenment to be, of all things, "the work of the devil." If that belief system weren't so destructive, it would actually be humorous. Unfortunately, the things we put our attention and energy on, we draw into our lives, so by energizing that belief, they create a great deal of chaos for themselves.

The New Age is not a religion; it is not a movement; it is not a particular belief or creed or philosophy. *The New Age is a span of time.* It is no more the "work of the devil" than a new day, a new month, a new season or a new year. An Age is a span of time that lasts approximately 2,000 years, and it is determined by some very physical, astronomical movements of the Planet just like our hours, days, months, seasons and years. Our hours and days change because of the Earth's daily rotation on her axis. The months, seasons and years change as a result of the Earth's annual revolution around the Sun and the constancy of the inclination of the Earth's axis throughout that orbit. The changing of the Age is due to an activity known as the "procession of the Equinox." As the Earth revolves daily on her axis and annually around the Sun, she also moves in a greater orbit through the twelve constellations that surround our Solar System. This orbit takes approximately 24,000 years.

Our Solar System is located in a particular time–space continuum. In the Universe surrounding our Solar System, there are twelve constellations which are referred to as the "natural zodiac." These constellations remain in the same general proximity to Earth, but because of the rotation of the Earth on her axis, each constellation has a period of time (approximately 32 degrees) or 2,000 years in which it has a predominant influence on the Planet.

Each spring, during the Vernal Equinox, the first degree of Aries is measured by the position of the Sun as it crosses the equator. This crossing point changes every year as the Earth moves in a gradual counterclockwise motion. The movement is very slight, only 50.2 seconds a year, but over time, the movement begins to add up. It takes approximately 72 years for the Earth to move one degree in her 360 degree 24,000 year orbit through the constellations. Remember, there are twelve constellations and 360 degrees in one complete 24,000 year orbit, so each constellation has a predominant influence on Earth for 32 degrees or 2,000 years.

As we complete one 32 degree cycle and move from the influence of one constellation into another, it is called a New Age. That is exactly what is happening on Earth at this time. We are completing the movement through the 32 degrees of Pisces, which lasted about 2,000 years, and we are entering the initial impulse of the 32 degrees of Aquarius, which will also last about 2,000 years.

THE WINDOW OF OPPORTUNITY IS NOW OPEN

When we move into the forcefield of a new constellation, it creates a monumental shift of energy on the Planet, and this shift in vibration allows a window of opportunity to open that enables higher frequencies of wisdom and understanding to pour into the consciousness of Humanity. This is easy to understand because all we have to do is observe the shift of energy that takes place on Earth when we have a full moon or a new moon. Look what happens when we have a sun spot flair up or when we experience a Solar or Lunar Eclipse. Even when a comet passes by, we feel the effects. It is really quite obvious that we are greatly affected by any change that occurs in the Heavenly bodies surrounding Earth. Just imagine how much more significant the change is when we move into the forcefield of an entirely different constellation.

Each of the twelve constellations vibrates with a different frequency of Light. These frequencies of Light are known as the twelve Solar Aspects of Deity. They contain specific Divine Qualities, colors, musical tones, fragrances, truths and understandings that are drawn from the Causal Body of God.

When the Earth moves into the forcefield of a new constellation, all of the gifts of Light from that particular constellation begin to pour into the Planet. The constellation of Aquarius reverberates with the Seventh Aspect of Deity. Contained within the vibrations of the Amethyst-Violet Light of the Seventh Ray or Seventh Aspect of Deity are the God Qualities of Forgiveness, Mercy, Compassion, Transmutation, Invocation, Rhythm and Freedom. This magnificent Violet Light will be the predominant influence on Planet Earth for the next 2,000 years. It has been decreed by Cosmic Fiat that, during this time period, the Earth will be transformed into her Divine Birthright which is Freedom's Holy Star. Spiritual Freedom, which means freedom in every facet of our lives, will be the blueprint of this New Age.

During the inception of each New Age, as the window of opportunity opens, God and the Legions of Light Who abide in the Heavenly Realms to do His Will, evaluate the progress

Humanity has made on Earth. It is then determined what assistance can be given from on High that will help Humanity and the other lifeforms evolving on Earth the most effectively on the journey Home to our Father-Mother God.

In Ages past, when the Earth was completely immersed in the humanly created discord of fear and confusion known as the veil of illusion, many attempts were made to raise the consciousness of Humanity. Very gradually greater levels of understanding trickled into Humanity's consciousness to help us regain our direction and to help us remember who we are, thus empowering us to accomplish our goal of loving this Planet free.

We know now that the "fall of man" and our perceived separation from God were self-inflicted. The existing negativity on Earth was never intended to be part of the Divine Plan. As we review briefly the occurrences that have taken place on Earth, bringing us to this Cosmic Moment, we will begin to awaken within our hearts the remembrance of why we are here at this critical time. Recorded deep within the cellular RNA-DNA factors of our beings is the memory of our Earthly sojourn and the knowledge of our purpose and reason for being here now. As the pre-encoded patterns of our Divine Plan are activated within us, we will begin to tap all of the experience, wisdom, talent, strength and courage we have developed over aeons of time to prime us for the Cosmic service we have volunteered to render to this precious Planet during this moment of transformation.

Prepare yourself now to read this information with an open mind and an open heart. I don't want you to ever accept something as truth just because someone has told you it's so. Invoke the Light of Illumined Truth and Divine Discernment through your being, and ask the Presence of God pulsating in your heart to filter out any trace of human consciousness. Ask that you be allowed to clearly recognize and accept only the truth that will set you free.

As we came forth from the Heart of God individualized as "I AM", we descended into denser and denser octaves of matter until we embodied on the physical plane of Earth. This is the process of INVOLUTION. As we proceeded through our Earthly sojourn, we were to develop and become masters of the material plane on our return journey back to the Heart of God. This is the process of EVOLUTION. Every particle of life, every electron of energy, is subject to this involutionary and evolutionary process.

Prior to the "fall of man," the Earth was a veritable Paradise. Everything that Humanity needed to exist in comfort and harmony had been provided by the Elemental Kingdom in cooperation with our God Parents. The human beings in embodiment at that time would draw forth their gift of life, the electronic Light substance we use continually with our every breath, and they would use it for the expansion of God's Will on Earth. This gift of life went forth from each person on an electro-magnetic current of energy similar to a radio wave. As each person sent forth their thoughts, words, feelings and actions, the current of energy would proceed into the physical plane and go directly to the person, place, condition or thing the sender was thinking of at the time. After reaching its point of destination, determined by the thought of the sender, the current of energy (our gift of life) would begin the return journey back to its Source, returning first to the person who sent it forth and then, back to the Heart of God. In the beginning, this gift of life was used only for good, and it was a continual blessing to all it touched.

The experiences reflecting in each person's life, as a result of the returning energy, qualified ONLY with the Will of God, were always joyous and mirrored the Perfection of God. This was the natural evolutionary process void of any trace of discord or negativity. This was the original Divine Plan for Earth and God's Will for all life. In order to insure this Divine process and to insure that our gift of free will would never be misused, God gave ONE commandment: "DO NOT PARTAKE OF THE TREE OF KNOWLEDGE OF GOOD AND EVIL."

As time passed, Humanity became curious about this commandment and eventually, through free will, chose to partake of the tree and "ate the apple." Upon doing so, for the very first time since we came forth from the Heart of God, we began to experiment with our gift of life in ways that were contrary to the Will of God. The currents of energy passing into the physical plane on our thoughts, words, feelings and actions no longer reflected just the Perfection of God. They were now tainted with the knowledge of evil. For the first time, Humanity began to experience vibrations that were discordant and contaminated with negativity.

As these discordant thoughts were projected into the atmosphere of Earth, they began to reflect on the environment. Gradually, the beauty of the Elemental Kingdom began to reflect decay and disease. Our physical bodies, comprised of the same elements, also began to show signs of aging and degeneration. Humanity, inexperienced and unfamiliar with the vibrations of discord, became perplexed and fearful. The glorious gift of life that used to flow so easily into the physical plane, qualified with God's Will, was now being misqualified by Humanity, and instead of pouring forth to bless all life, it went forth from each person as a heavy inharmonious current. It then proceeded to the person, place, condition or thing held in the sender's thoughts, causing pain and friction along the way. After reaching its point of destination, it returned to the sender on its journey home to the Source.

But now there was a flaw. The energy could not pass through the sender's heart on its return to God because it was contaminated and no longer vibrated with God's Will. The Law is, that in order for our gift of life to return to the Source, it must be vibrating with the same or a higher frequency than when it is first received. Now a greater problem ensued. Since the returning negative energy could not return to the Source until it had been transmuted back into Light, and since Humanity didn't have the understanding or knowledge of how to accomplish that purification, the destructive energy had no where to go and had to remain in the atmosphere of Earth. Gradually, as time passed, a cloud of negativity began to form around the Planet. It became denser and denser, creating a veil of maya or illusion blinding Humanity from the truth of our God reality and our purpose for being. This greatly added to the complexity of the problem.

Once Humanity lost the awareness of our God reality and our purpose for being, we became more confused and frightened, consequently creating more negativity until the end result, known as "the fall of man," manifested on Earth. During this dark period of time, we separated ourselves from God so severely that today–millions of years later–we are still struggling to reconnect with our God Presence, and we are striving to transmute the sea of negativity surrounding the Planet that is known as the humanly created psychic-astral realm.

In retrospect, it is clear why God gave a commandment "not to partake of the tree of knowledge of good and evil." Our gift of free will is a sacred trust given to us by God and interpenetrates all realms of knowledge. God will *not* interfere with our free will REGARDLESS of how we choose to use it. Without the knowledge of evil we would not have been tempted to misqualify our gift of life, but once we partook of the fruit of that tree, we were subject to all the ramifications of that knowledge.

Evil, as we experience it on Earth, involves any frequency of vibration that does not emulate the harmony and balance of Divine Love. God does not release one electron of energy that is less than the frequency of perfection. Therefore, *anything* taking place on Earth that is less than God's Perfection of Divine Love is our own human creation, and it is in conflict with God's Will. It is a result of misqualifying our gift of life and the abuse of our creative faculties of thought and feeling.

The Law of the Universe is balance, and when a planet and the evolutions evolving on the planet utilize the gift of life from God, they are responsible for how they use every electron. It is a Cosmic Law that in order for God to continue breathing life into a planetary system, the lifestreams using that gift of life must expand the gift adding to the Light of the world as it returns to our Father-Mother God. This is the balance of the Inbreath and the Outbreath of all life.

When the Earth had fallen to her darkest ebb, we were not emanating the necessary balance of Light to warrant our gift of life. At that point, God determined that the Light must be withdrawn from the Planet, thereby allowing all the lifeforms on Earth to disintegrate and return to unformed primal substance. When the knowledge of this decision reached the Spiritual Hierarchy, Who selflessly serve the Planet Earth, an urgent plea and clarion call rang through the Universe. The Spiritual Hierarchy pleaded with God and all the Legions of Light throughout this System of Worlds to allow Divine Intervention in the salvation of this fallen star. Through that plea, a Cosmic Dispensation was granted and a span of time allotted to see if Earth could regain her path. The Spiritual Hierarchy invoked the assistance of the entire Universe, and from Galaxies beyond Galaxies and Suns beyond Suns, the greatest unified effort of Divine Love ever manifested in the history of time was projected forth into this small dark star.

Whenever there is a significant amount of energy released for a particular purpose, God evaluates the situation and decides if additional grants of energy or assistance can be allowed. In this case, it was evident that there was enough desire from the Universe, if not Humanity, to warrant the salvation of this precious Planet. Again, a Cosmic Dispensation was granted, and it was agreed that the Planet Earth would survive, and additional assistance would be permitted to awaken the Divinity within Humanity in order to heal our separation from God.

Several Ages ago the first major plan to raise the consciousness of Humanity was implemented. During the opening of the window of opportunity for that particular Age, an unusual experiment was tried. It was hoped that if Humanity could live with and observe highly evolved souls, we would remember our own Divinity, and we would learn how to attain our potential as human beings, regaining our path. A unique dispensation was granted, and as souls evolved into Ascended Beings, instead of lifting into Fourth Dimensional frequencies, beyond the physical sight of Humanity, as they had done in the past, they were allowed to remain on Earth as examples to show us our human potential. Unfortunately, we misunderstood their message, and instead of aspiring to Godliness ourselves, we began to separate ourselves from them and deify them. We expected them to do for us the very things they were trying to teach us to do for ourselves. We worshipped them, and instead of being a benefit to our growth, they became a distraction. Historically, this is the time when the so called gods and goddesses walked on Earth. This is the period referred to in Greek Mythology.

When it was determined by God that this experiment had failed, the Ascended Beings raised their vibratory rate into the Octaves of the Fourth Dimension and disappeared from physical sight. It was hard for future generations to conceive that Beings of that level of consciousness actually existed on Earth, so they surmised that they must be a myth.

When the Ascended Beings vanished from sight, Humanity became frightened and tried to replace them with false idols. Large statues were created and worshiped throughout the Planet.

When the window of opportunity opened again as the frequencies of the next Age began to be felt on Earth, a new plan was set into motion. It was clearly seen by the Heavenly Realms that Humanity was so deeply immersed in the darkness of our own self-created negativity that the veil of illusion surrounding the Planet had effectively blocked the Light from "above." The veil was blinding us from the truth of our own God reality. We felt cut off from our Source, and as we looked at the world through the eyes of our foggy, limited perception, we believed that the physical plane of Earth was all that existed.

It was obvious at that point, if Humanity was going to progress, we needed to again remember where we came from and reunite with our Source. In order for this to happen, it was imperative that the Light of God reach the Earth once more. Several very illumined souls volunteered to come to Earth to open portals through the sea of negativity surrounding the Planet so the Light could again shine on Earth. A succession of Avatars and Buddhas appeared on the screen of life, and the knowledge and wisdom of Eastern religions began to register in the consciousness of Humanity. Meditation became a spiritual practice enabling Humanity to reach up in vibration, piercing through the veil of the psychic-astral plane into the Realms of Illumined Truth. This process opened pathways over which the Light of God could once again shine on Earth.

When people go through the near death experience, they describe passing through a dark tunnel into the Light. This dark tunnel is a passage through the psychic-astral realm. The difference between what the Buddhas and Avatars accomplished and what occurs naturally during death is that in death souls leave the Earth Plane permanently and withdraw their lifeforce with them. Consequently, the pathway closes behind them as they pass into the Light. But in meditation, the souls remain anchored in the physical realm on Earth and thus maintain the opening so the Light can reach the third dimensional planes again.

This plan had a degree of success, but even with the increased influx of Light, Humanity still had a belief in false idols and multi-deity. When the next Age began to reverberate through the ethers and the window of opportunity appeared, it was determined by God that Humanity needed to again learn of the Oneness of God and eliminate the worship of false idols. As this wisdom began to reach the minds of Humanity, the Sacred Doctrine of Judaism was written. Monotheism became the order of the day, and false idols were rejected. We began to understand the reality of One God, but in our limited understanding, we still felt very separated from God. We considered God angry and wrathful. We believed Him to be a punishing God, and we believed He was to be feared. This misconception prevented us from healing our self-inflicted separation from God, and it perpetuated the belief that "man is a worm in the dust."

Needless to say, as the next window of opportunity appeared, much work needed to be done. At that moment in time, we were moving into the forcefield of Pisces and the frequencies of the Sixth Solar Aspect of Deity. The God Qualities associated with this Ruby Ray are Ministering Grace,

Peace, Healing and Devotional Worship. God evaluated the state of Humanity and clearly ascertained that it was time for us to experience the reality of God and the love of God in a tangible, personal way. A beautiful illumined soul, known to us as Jesus, volunteered to come to Earth to reveal to Humanity the reality of our own Divinity, to prove in manifest form that we are truly Sons and Daughters of God, to confirm our Oneness with God and to lead us Home through the pathway of Christ Consciousness which heals our separation from God. As we lift into Christ Consciousness, we experience the realization of our own Resurrection and Ascension into the Light.

Beloved Jesus continually affirmed throughout His mission of Ministering Grace, "Ye are Gods."

Jesus answered them, "Is it not written in your law, I said, "YE ARE GODS?"

JOHN 10:34

"YE ARE GODS; and all of you ARE children of the most High."

PSALM 82:1-6

"Verily, verily, I say unto you, he that believeth in me the works that I do shall he do also, AND EVEN GREATER WORKS THAN THESE SHALL HE DO..."

JOHN 14:12

"For as many as are led by the Spirit of God, they are the sons of God—the spirit itself beareth witness with our spirit that we are the children of God; and if children, then heirs, heirs of God, JOINT HEIRS WITH CHRIST.."

ROMANS 8:14, 16, 17

"When I consider Thy heavens, the work of Thy fingers, the moon and the stars which Thou hast ordained; what is man, that Thou art mindful of him and the son of man, that Thou visitest him? For Thou hast made him a little lower than the angels, and has crowned him with glory and honor. Thou madest him TO HAVE DOMINION OVER THE WORKS OF THY HANDS; THOU HAST PUT ALL THINGS UNDER HIS FEET."

PSALMS 8:3-6

Even though Jesus continually reiterated our worth and

stated, "It is not I, but the Father within Who does the work," we still misunderstood his message, and once again separated ourselves from him, deified him and worshiped him.

Jesus came as a manifest example of what each and every one of us is destined to become. He utilized the frequencies of the New Age of Pisces to accomplish his mission. His symbol was the fish, which is the symbol of Pisces, and he was known as the Prince of Peace which expanded the Light of the Sixth Aspect of Deity. He entered the Earth during the opening of the window of opportunity that occurs at the inception of each New Age. He sought out the wisdom of the Ages during his 18 missing years, and after he applied the truth of God to his life, he passed quickly through his initiations into Christhood. Through this personal victory, he unified with the flow of the Universal Presence of God, "I AM", which enabled him to accomplish his complete avatarship for the entire 2,000 year cycle of the Sixth Ray Christian Dispensation of Pisces in just THREE SHORT YEARS.

We are now at the end of the Piscean Age, and the New Age of Aquarius is dawning. We, like Jesus, have entered the Earth during the opening of the window of opportunity. The frequencies of Light, wisdom and understanding pouring into the consciousness of Humanity now are unparalleled in the history of time. The "I Am" Presence has returned to Earth through the consciousness of the Christ, and neither time, nor space, nor circumstances can block the flow of Its perfection to Earth. We are destined to become millions and millions of magnificent Christ Beings whose brilliant Light illumines and transforms the Planet in just a few short years. But, as it was for Beloved Jesus, our inner preparation is the key in order for the Divine Plan to be brought to fruition according to schedule. There are awesome events taking place on Earth that are moving us forward in quantum leaps and bounds. Never before has Humanity been given such assistance. Never before have we had such an opportunity to quickly move through our challenges and into the Octaves of Blissful Harmony and Balance. The awakening is occurring through the activation of the pre-encoded memories within our cellular structures, and we are beginning to know from deep within our hearts, "I AM" the open door which no one can shut. "I AM" the Light of the world, and my time is at hand!

During the opening of the window of opportunity for the dawning Age of Aquarius, God and the entire Company of Heaven have again evaluated the need of the hour. Things are very different this time. There is a greater urgency. It is no longer a matter of just restoring the Earth to her original path, but now the entire Galaxy is involved. From Cosmic Law, it has been decreed that the time has come for our Solar System, along with the rest of the Solar Systems in our Galaxy, to advance to a higher sphere of Cosmic Evolution. This is a natural part of the evolutionary process that occurs in all Planetary Systems every several billion years or so. As a Solar System is breathed out from the Heart of our Father-Mother God, it is projected into the Universe to its furthest point of destination–this is Involution. Then, as the Solar System evolves, it is gradually breathed back into the Heart of God as it Ascends step by step back to its Source–this is Evolution. Our Universe is now in the process of being breathed in another evolutionary step on our return journey Home. At this time, the progress and state of consciousness of each Planet in our System of Worlds is being evaluated by God. The Planets that have evolved sufficiently will qualify for the advancement, but those that are found wanting in the final grading will be left behind to be repolarized and returned to primal substance, thus ending their opportunity for individualization.

During the Earth's evaluation, it was obvious that, even though we have received Cosmic Dispensations in Ages past to lift us out of darkness, our progress has been painfully slow. It has taken thousands of years to bring us to this point, and still we have just begun to scratch the surface of what we must do to regain our direction. During God's evaluation of Earth, it became clear that recalcitrant Humanity couldn't possibly accomplish, in the short time left, what needed to be done in order for Earth to be able to make the move into the next sphere of Cosmic Evolution. Once again, Earth faced impending dissolution. The Spiritual Hierarchy serv-

ing Earth realized They would receive little help from the
limited awareness of Humanity, so the clarion call rang out
to the Cosmos for help. The heartfelt response was beyond
Their greatest expectations, and assistance came, once
again, from Galaxies beyond Galaxies and Suns beyond
Suns. Illumined souls, beyond any that have ever inhabited
the Earth, volunteered to come and embody on Earth to assist in awakening Humanity. Permission was granted by the
Karmic Board, and thousands upon thousands of illumined
souls began incarnating on Earth in every conceivable corner
of the globe. They have chosen to embody into every walk of
life, every country, every nationality, every socio-economic
state, every culture, every religion, every government and
every facet of Earthly experience. Many of them have chosen
to come into crash courses because they never experienced
anything like the negativity on Earth. Some have chosen
poverty, disfunctional families, disease, abuse, failure,
famine, war and all manner of Earthly suffering. They understand the Cosmic Law, "As I am lifted up, all life is lifted
up with me." Therefore, they have volunteered to enter into
the depths of the frequencies of despair on Earth, knowing
full well that, as they lift into the Light, they will lift those
frequencies of hopelessness with them.

No matter how evolved a soul is, when a being volunteers
to embody in a particular Planetary System, he/she is subject
to all of the Laws of that System. On Earth, because of the
confusion and the accumulated negativity existing here, we
are given at birth what is known as the "band of forgetfulness." This band suppresses our memory of the past and enables us to focus on the present. Currently, we are being
given the opportunity to transmute, literally, hundreds of
past lifetimes in a very short time. If we remembered all of
the pain and suffering that is surfacing now to clear, it would
be unbearable, and we wouldn't be able to stand it. This
band is truly a merciful gift, and we will one day appreciate
it for the compassionate service it has rendered to us. But in
the meantime, we feel frustrated by it because it also prevents us from remembering who we are and why we are here.

The illumined souls who have come to Earth to assist in

loving this Planet free have been given the band of forgetfulness also. They do not consciously remember who they are, and it is not obvious in any way that they have come from other dimensions and Star Systems to help, but they have some telltale signs in common.

1. They have a deep affinity to God and all Divinity.
2. They feel there is something very important they must do to help Humanity and the Earth, even if they don't know exactly what it is yet.
3. They often feel shy about expressing it, but they know they are very powerful and can make a difference.
4. They are sensing the urgency of the hour.
5. They are feeling the time is *now*, and they must begin to fulfill their highest potential.
6. They realize all life is interrelated, and they recognize our Oneness.
7. They feel deep compassion for Humanity's suffering and the suffering of Mother Earth and the kingdom of nature.
8. They know we are in the process of momentus change, and they feel the joy of expectancy.
9. In the midst of the negativity surfacing on the screen of life, they are still hopeful and enthusiastic, and they have absolute confidence in the success of planetary transformation.
10. They know we are multi-dimensional beings and readily commune with the Octaves of Light in prayer and meditation.
11. They are aware of the power of the unified consciousness of Humanity and organize and participate in global activities of planetary healing.
12. They are experiencing an awakening taking place within themselves. They know they have come to love this Planet free, and as they guide Humanity and all life into the Light, so they shall.

DIVINE DISCERNING INTELLIGENCE

If *any* of the above information resonates as truth within your heart of hearts, know that this is not just a coincidence. It is time for you to begin fulfilling your Divine Plan, time for you to recognize who you are and what you have come to do. This inner knowing, however, is a gift and a sacred trust. It is to be held in the silence of your heart, and through the example and radiance of your Presence, will your work be accomplished.

Sometimes people will get a glimpse of who they are before they tap the wisdom of spiritual discernment to handle such information. A lot of the confusion about the New Age is a result of this phenomenon. Nowadays, it's not uncommon to be in a social situation and ask someone where they are from and hear a response like, "I'm a walk-in from the Pleiades." Instead of enhancing our ability to serve, this kind of remark discredits us, and people become suspicious, not only of our integrity, but of our sanity.

In order for us to truly be of help to our fellow human beings, we need to be "normal." We need to set our egos aside and remember that the only way this Planet is going to evolve is for every man, woman and child to aspire to their highest potential.

We do not inspire people to greater levels of attainment by separating ourselves from them and making ourselves an oddity. Nor do we inspire them with the "holier than thou" attitude, that we are special and have come to save them. The most effective Lightworkers are securely anchored at a grassroots level in mainstream Humanity, successfully functioning every day in all the various walks of life, proving through their life experience the Laws of Abundance, Love, Joy, Happiness, Health, Success, Victory, Freedom and all of the other attributes of God. Remember, the truth of the admonition of the false prophets is, "Lo, I am here, and Lo, I am there, but by their works alone shall they be known."

As the pre-encoded memories of the truth of your being are activated within you, ask your God Presence to also give you the spiritual discernment to utilize the information in a way that will reflect only the highest good for you and all concerned. Instead of professing how wonderful we are with empty words, it's time to actually "walk our talk" as the expression goes. It's time to *"Be still and know..."*

Because of the urgency of the hour, Earth is receiving assistance in the form of Divine Intervention beyond anything that has ever been experienced in any system of worlds. The hundreds of thousands, possibly millions, of illumined souls embodied on Earth now are awakening. We have been prepared to reach up into the Realms of Truth and tap the Divine Mind of God as we join forces with the entire Company of Heaven. We are being asked to listen to the still, small voice of our God Presence that resonates in our hearts and grasp intelligently the need of the hour so that we can whole-heartedly cooperate with the Spiritual Hierarchy Who have been granted permission to come through the veil to meet us half way.

Over the past 50 years, the Beings of Light Who abide in the Heavenly Realms to do God's Will have directed and guided us through some unparalleled changes. God needs a "body," however, and even the grandest plan of Heaven is destined to failure if there aren't lifestreams in the physical plane willing to implement that plan. I would like to share with you some of the things that have transpired over the past few years. These momentus events have brought us to this Cosmic Moment and laid the foundation for the quantum leaps we are going to take now. Read this information with an open mind and an open heart, and you will begin to understand why it was stated in the Bible that the transformation will take place "in the twinkling of an eye."

BE BALANCED IN YOUR DIVINITY

In order for us to evolve into the Divine Sons and Daughters of God we are destined to be, it is necessary that we be balanced in the Divine Spark pulsating in our hearts.

This Spark of Divinity is known as the Immortal Victorious Three-fold Flame. It reflects the Divine Balance of the three-fold activity of life which is Love, Wisdom and Power, and it is the expression of life we have come to know as the Holy Trinity–the Father, the Son and Holy Spirit (Mother).

This Divine Flame contains within its frequencies the Masculine Polarity of God which is the Blue Flame of Divine Will and Power, the Feminine Polarity of God which is the Pink Flame of Divine Love and the Son/Daughter Principle of God which is the Yellow-Gold Flame of Wisdom and Enlightenment, often referred to as the Christ. When these three activities of Love, Wisdom and Power are balanced within us, we express the necessary harmony through our creative faculties of thought and feeling to create lives of joy and perfection.

The Masculine Polarity of God, the Blue Flame of Power, activates our left brain hemisphere. This is our rational, logical mind, the center which enables us to think practically and analytically. The Masculine Polarity of Power also expresses through the energy vortex of our throat, the power center known as the throat chakra, and it expands out through our hands directing our action in the world of form.

The Feminine Polarity of God, the Pink Flame of Divine Love, activates our right brain hemisphere. This is our creative, intuitive mind, the center which enables us to love, feel, envision, dream and express emotions. The Feminine Polarity of Divine Love also expresses through the energy vortex of our heart, the heart chakra.

In order for us to express our full potential, it is imperative that our right and left brain hemispheres, our faculties of power and love, be balanced. When the Masculine Polarity of God and the Feminine Polarity of God, the right and left hemispheres of the brain, are balanced, it results in the activation of the pituitary and pineal centers which awaken the energy vortex within the brain known as the crown chakra, the center of wisdom, enlightenment, understanding and illumination... in other words, the consciousness of the Christ.

When these three activities are balanced:

HEART	–	HEAD	–	HAND
LOVE	–	WISDOM	–	POWER
RIGHT BRAIN	–	CHRIST CONSCIOUSNESS	–	LEFT BRAIN

we automatically use our creative faculties of thought and feeling in alignment with God's Will and the Divine Plan on Earth.

Unfortunately, with the "fall of man," we lost sight of this truth. We began using our power without balancing it with love. When we balance power with love, we always express a reverence for life, and we remain in a state of illumined Christ Consciousness that enables us to see viable solutions and options to our Earthly challenges other than aggression, dominance, corruption and force. All we have to do is observe the human conditions existing on Earth today to know that our power centers are grossly and destructively out of balance.

This imbalance has been our nemisis since the first traces of the "fall" occurred on the continent of Lemuria, sometimes called Mu, in the Pacific Ocean. When the souls evolving on that continent had fallen to the epitomy of degradation, it was determined by God that the land mass must sink below the healing waters of the ocean to be purged.

After the purging of Lemuria, new civilizations began evolving on the continent of Atlantis in the Atlantic Ocean. Unfortunately, after developing to high levels of attainment, once again the power center was used without the balance of love. Through the abuse of power, the eventual purging of Atlantis also became the Fiat of Divinity. The final island of Atlantis, named Poseidonis, sank below the healing waters about 10,000 years B.C.

Since that time, we have experienced this dire scenerio over and over again. Every single imbalance existing on Earth can be traced to some form of abuse of our power, some thought, feeling or action that did not reflect Divine Love or reverence for all life.

BALANCING THE FEMININE POLARITY
OF DIVINE LOVE

It is obvious that bringing the Feminine Polarity of Divine Love into balance on Earth *is the critical key* to planetary transformation. This is the ambition of all of the Divine Beings in Heaven and Earth at this moment. In 1954, a Cosmic push to accelerate this process began.

There is a tremendous shaft of the Blue Flame of the Masculine Polarity of God that enters the forcefield of the Himalayan Mountains in Tibet, and there is a tremendous shaft of the Pink Flame of the Feminine Polarity of God that enters the forcefield of the Andes Mountains in Mt. Muru in South America. These two Divine Polarities meet in the center of the Earth, and at the point of union, the Son/Daughter Principle of Christ Light is born. This forms the Immortal Victorious Three-fold Flame for the Planet in the center of the Earth. This Three-fold Flame is sometimes called the Sun of Even Pressure at Earth's core.

In 1954, our Father-Mother God and the entire Company of Heaven began projecting greater frequencies of Divine Love through the Feminine Polarity of God anchored in the Andes Mountains. This Light increased in momentum gently and effectively for 33 years. Thirty-three is the mystical number that symbolizes the manifestation of Christ Consciousness. During this time, many important things were revealed to those among Humanity who could hear the voice of the God Presence within, and many crucial steps were taken to assist in the expansion of the Feminine Aspect of Divine Love on Earth.

One of the most severe blocks to the expansion of Light on the Planet was a tear in the etheric garment of Earth. It was revealed by the Realms of Truth that the sinking of Lemuria was so catastrophic that the process actually caused a tear in the etheric body of Mother Earth, creating a vacuum that trapped hundreds of thousands of souls in a veritable limbo or time warp. These souls from Lemuria had to be freed, and the etheric tear healed before the Earth could absorb more Light and ascend in frequency of vibration. After much preparation and many sacred ceremonies of healing, the tear was healed in 1983, and the trapped souls freed to continue their evolutionary process in the schools of learning in inner realms.

THE WORLD HEALING MEDITATION

The success of this healing allowed the frequencies of Divine Love to be amplified on Earth. This influx of Light increased the vibratory rate of the Planet gradually and began activating the pre-encoded memories within the illumined souls in embodiment. An awakening started taking place within Humanity, and we began to remember why we are here. The concepts of unified consciousness and global service became practical, logical experiences. Lightworkers began to take action in every country on Earth. Networking became the order of the day, and we began to unite, even in our diversity. We began to understand more clearly than ever before that we each have a unique thread to weave into the tapestry of life on Earth, and each of our threads is equally significant and necessary. Socially conscious organizations, geared to planetary healing and transformation, began springing up everywhere. We began to truly understand that the unified consciousness of Humanity is the most powerful force on Earth. To take advantage of that power, the Lightworkers started to join their efforts in global meditations. The word spread quickly, and after a few short years of preparation, on December 31, 1986, the greatest unified activity of planetary healing ever known on Earth took place. An estimated 500 million Lightworkers from all over the world joined together in prayer and meditation at 12:00 Noon, Greenwich Mean Time, to invoke the healing of Beloved Mother Earth. The cup of our unified consciousness allowed the Feminine Polarity of Divine Love to be amplified beyond anything we had experienced since prior to the fall of man. Through this sacred activity of Light, this Planet ascended a quantum leap into the frequencies of harmony. This prepared the Earth for the next great influx of Light.

HARMONIC CONVERGENCE

After the shift of vibration took place during the World Healing Meditation, many more Lightworkers began to awaken. An eminent activity of global significance began to filter into the consciousness of Humanity. We began to sense the need to reach higher into the Realms of Truth. As we did, more information was revealed, and the opportunity at hand was recognized. The impending event was referred to in the outer world as Harmonic Convergence, and it occurred on August 15th, 16th and 17th in 1987. This was the cosmic moment the entire Company of Heaven had been preparing for for 33 years. This was the moment when the Feminine Polarity of God's Divine Love would, once again, be brought into balance in the Realms of Cause where it would be anchored permanently to gradually reflect into the everyday lives of the people on Earth.

When the Feminine Polarity of God and the Masculine Polarity of God are brought into perfect balance, it results in the birthing of the Son/Daughter principle of God which is the Christ Light of Enlightenment. During the unique moment of Harmonic Convergence when the Feminine Polarity of God reached the point of perfect balance in the Realms of Cause, the Sunshine Yellow Light of Enlightenment began flowing into the Earth. This Light of pure Christ Consciousness was absorbed into the Heart Flames of Lightworkers who had gathered at sacred sights all over the Planet. As the Christ Light of Enlightenment was breathed from their Heart Flames into the physical plane, it was projected into the crystal grid system of Earth. This is the energy system of the Planet, the actual acupuncture meridians through which Light is transmitted into the physical body of Earth. This process began the initial reactivation of the crystal grid system and accelerated the frequency of vibration of all life evolving on Earth into a higher Octave of Light. This occurred at an atomic, cellular level through every particle of life.

We were told by the Realms of Truth that Harmonic Convergence was the initial impulse of a transformational process that would take 25 years to complete. The Heavenly Realms informed us that the first five years would be the most difficult and the most tumultuous. Then, there would be a planetary shift that would move us closer to the Heart of our Father-Mother God, making the next 20 years easier as we ascend into the Light moment by moment the maximum Cosmic Law will allow.

If we reflect on the things that have taken place on Earth since Harmonic Convergence, it will be impossible for us to deny the fact that we are definitely and absolutely on the path of transformation. One of the things that occurs as the frequencies of Divine Love increase in the physical plane is that anything existing here that conflicts with Divine Love is pushed to the surface to be cleared. This is causing some extreme imbalances. Any facet of life, personal, political, economic, etc., that is not based in integrity and reverence for life is being exposed in the Light of Truth, and if it isn't corrected, it will crumble and disintegrate. This is usually very uncomfortable, and that is why this particular time frame, referred to in the Bible as the latter days, is known as the time of "the screaming and the gnashing of teeth."

To confirm this statement, just reflect for a few minutes on the things that have been occurring in your life. Any area where you are not reaching your highest potential is being pushed to the surface in such a way that you don't have any choice but to look at it and deal with it. What area is coming up for you? Is it self-esteem issues? Finances? Relationships? Health? Opportunities to allow you to deal with your past? Job or career issues? Substance abuse? Co-dependence? Other addictions? Failure? All of the above? Observe how these things seem to have been amplified in the last few years, and notice how you can no longer just stuff them back down again the way you used to.

Fortunately, with the accelerated influx of Light, even though these things surfacing are uncomfortable, we also have more information on how to handle the challenges. We understand that things are coming up, not to plague or punish us, but to give us an opportunity to clear them once and for all, so we can really create lives of joy and abundance for ourselves. There are now new, wonderful, innovative tools available to help us. It is not intended that this process of purification be overwhelming or unbearable. That is why greater wisdom and insight on the process of clearing our past and regaining our direction toward our highest potential and our Divine Plan are readily available.

With the shift that took place through all life during Harmonic Convergence, our four lower bodies–physical, etheric, mental and emotional were raised up in vibration, closer to the frequencies of our "I AM" Presence, our true God reality. Prior to the fall of man, our God Presence effectively functioned through our four lower bodies, but when we became immersed in the discord of our own negativity, our four lower bodies sank in vibration into the chasm of the veil of illusion. This was the greatest tragedy of the fall. This was our self-inflicted separation from our own Divinity.

Along the spinal column of our physical body we have seven major chakras or energy vortexes that transmit energy through the acupuncture meridians into our cells and organs, thus enabling us to survive in physical form. But, along the spinal column of our "I AM" Presence, there are twelve Solar chakras that transmit the Divine Qualities of the twelve Solar Aspects of Deity into the world of form. With the separation, we lost the ability to receive and transmit the Solar frequencies of Divinity through our physical chakras into the third dimensional plane.

With the balancing of the Feminine Polarity of Divine Love in the Realms of Cause and with the influx of the Christ Light of Enlightenment, our physical spine was raised up in vibration closer to the Solar Spine of our God Presence. Step by step, we are beginning to resonate with the twelve Solar Aspects of Deity, and as our transformation proceeds, we will experience more and more of the qualities of Divinity in our daily lives. Then, the Universal Law of "As above, so below" will again be a reality.

Just for a moment, close your eyes and visualize this unifying activity of Light.

"I AM" ONE WITH GOD AND ONE WITH HUMANITY

Breathing slowly and rhythmically, I begin to lift in consciousness beyond the physical plane into the Realms of Illumined Truth. In these frequencies of perfection, I see the glory of God's Light and the radiant colors of the twelve Solar Aspects of Deity. I hear the Music of the Spheres, and "I AM" calm and peaceful. I feel the bliss of Divinity, for I have ascended through the consciousness of my Holy Christ Self into the greater consciousness of "I AM". In this Presence and Being, I realize that the Twelve-fold Solar Spine of my God Presence anchors as a great shaft of Light through my physical body. It is the manifest expression of the finger of God Almighty entering Planet Earth from the Realms of Perfection saying "Here... 'I AM'." I see the twelve Solar chakras blazing along this shaft of Solar Fire. I accept and know that this Divine Presence is Who I truly am. Into the radiance of my Twelve-fold Solar Spine I now gently assimilate my seven-fold planetary spine, and I realize as never before "I AM" both of these natures. "I AM" a multi-dimensional Being. "I AM" both Solar and planetary, Divine and human, for "I AM" my Holy Christ Self... the Divine Mediator between God and Humanity. I understand clearly now that this is what Beloved Jesus meant when He stated "it is only through me (meaning the Christ) that you return to the Father." I know I serve through a planetary body, but I dwell in the consciousness of my great "I AM" Presence.

In this accelerated consciousness of "I AM", I realize "I

AM" a shaft of Light projected out of the Fourth Dimensional Realms of Perfection. "I AM" a bridge anchoring this Planet and Humanity into that Octave of Light. Through my inner sight, I see millions of such shafts of Light anchoring through the Lightworkers in Humanity, and I know that God Almighty has reached out to claim this Earth. I now see horizontal shafts of Light, blazing from Heart Flame to Heart Flame through all Lightworkers on Earth, uniting all embodied anchorage points of Light, establishing a mighty planetary forcefield of Divine Love and Security, a grid system of Light throughout Humanity which embraces this blessed Planet in the invincible arms of God's Protection.

"I AM" now able to effectively dwell in the twelve-fold consciousness of my Solar Presence "I AM" even as I serve in this seven-fold body of planetary existence. "I AM" at peace with this duality of my Christ nature. "I AM" one with God and one with Humanity.

Visualization from Group Avatar

Now, gently return your consciousness to the room, remaining in this elevated state of awareness, as we continue our discussion.

EARTH-LINK 88

Once we began to reunite with our God Presence and the Planet was embraced in a forcefield of security and love, it was possible for steps of tremendous magnitude to be taken to assist in moving us forward into the Light.

On February 13th, 1988, an event called Earth-Link 88 took place. It was the next major shift of vibration on Earth. The interim period between Harmonic Convergence and Earth-Link 88 represented a turning point in the direction of world endeavor. A shift in frequency from deception and corruption to honesty and integrity began occurring on Earth, and the Universal Law—"all that is hidden must now be revealed"—began reverberating through the ethers. This shift in vibration created the October 17, 1987, crash of the stock market and exposed the corruption existing in our entire economic and political systems. There is now a level of accountability required of political and corporate structure that was not previously in existence. This will gradually increase until only those individuals and organizations who are working toward the highest good for all concerned and functioning with their power centers balanced with love will be successful.

The critical mass which balanced the Feminine Polarity of Divine Love in causal levels of creation during Harmonic Convergence was externalized as an explosion of Light on February 13, 1988. People everywhere experienced a resonate shift in their level of conscious awareness. A collective ceiling of human thought opened to the Spiritual Realms of the Fourth Dimension allowing a stream of Light to enter each person's sphere of consciousness. This process amplified the awakening taking place on Earth and illuminated a vision of Higher Truth. Pure Light was projected from the Heart of God through the core of purity that pulsates in every created atom and from within every living cell in the human body, thus restructuring the genetic blueprint with higher life codes. This activity of Light increased the awakening of Humanity as our "I AM" consciousness was brought into alignment with the Universal Presence of God "I AM" That "I AM". Light then increased moment to moment on the Planet, enabling the Seventh Angelic Vortex to be opened.

STAR∗LINK 88

On June 11, 1988, through an event called Star∗Link 88, a dimensional doorway was opened, and the Seventh Angelic

Vortex was activated in the City of Angels at the Los Angeles Coliseum in California.

Several thousand lifestreams gathered together during a six-hour event of unified consciousness in which a reactivation and initiation into multi-dimensional awareness occurred. This blessed Planet and ALL Her life were lifted up yet another octave in vibration, closer to the Heart of our Father-Mother God.

Through the activity of Star✶Link 88, the Angelic Host, from frequencies beyond anything we have ever experienced, entered the atmosphere of Earth. These mighty Seraphim from the Fifth Dimension assisted God in activating the pre-encoded memories that were implanted deep within Humanity's cellular patterns aeons ago. These patterns reflect our Divine Plan, our purpose and reason for being. Humanity will now experience a great soaring and awakening as we begin to remember our Divine Heritage.

A Cosmic Fiat was issued by God, and 1988 was decreed the year in which Humanity would step through the doorway into multi-dimensional awareness. This was accomplished as the frequencies of the third dimension were accelerated closer to the higher Octaves of the Fourth Dimension.

During that sacred moment in time, Humanity was empowered with the increased presence of the Angelic Host which is, even now, continually entering the Earth through the Seventh Angelic Vortex. The influx of Angels has formed an expanded bridge between Heaven and Earth–spirit and matter. Over this Sacred Bridge, the Rays of Light of the Twelve-fold Aspect of Deity from The Great Central Sun perpetually bathe the Earth.

The Light from these Ministering Angels is increasing daily and hourly. Moment to moment the activated, pre-encoded memories of our purpose and reason for being, now reflecting at a physical, cellular level within our four lower bodies, are reverberating through our creative centers of thought and feeling. As these currents of wisdom and illumination pass through our conscious minds, our God Presence sends a Ray of Light to help us tangibly grasp each Divine idea. Knowledge of our Divine Plan is now available to us as never before. We need only reach up and tap the Octaves of Illumined Truth.

Lightworkers throughout the Planet continue to awaken daily, and the body of world servers referred to as Group Avatar is ever growing.

In a rhythmic momentum on the anniversaries of the World Healing Meditation, Harmonic Convergence, the Solstices and Equinoxes, the new moons and the full moons, Lunar and Solar Eclipses and the sacred holidays of all world religions, Lightworkers join together in global activities invoking the Light through prayer and meditation to assist this sweet Earth in her process of rebirth.

CRYSTAL LIGHTLINK

In 1989 some events of tremendous magnitude took place. On April 16, 1989, an activity called Crystal Lightlink occurred. During that unique moment, God projected into the crystal grid system of Earth unparalleled frequencies of the Twelve-fold Aspect of Deity. This activity of Light accelerated the awakening taking place on the Planet. The energies initiated a massive planetary and galactic activation and reprogramming of all crystalline structures existing within the Earth, the etheric plane and within the human body. This activation raised the consciousness of every soul and every living cell on Earth.

The activated crystal system on Earth was then able to function at a higher level of effectiveness, transmitting energy like our crystal radio sets of the past or our quartz crystal watches. This event greatly enhanced our telecommunication system with interdimensional, interstellar, intergalactic energies and with higher intelligences.

SEALING THE DOOR WHERE EVIL DWELLS

With the activation accelerated, other doors of opportunity began to open. In May of 1989, awakened Humanity began to perceive more clearly their ability to work in conscious cooperation with the Spiritual Hierarchy Who serve Earth from the Realms of Illumined Truth. This awareness enabled a plan to be implemented from "On High" to purge the Earth of the pockets of negativity that existed in various vortexes on the Planet. These negative vortexes had been created over aeons of time and were sustained and energized by the fallen souls known as the forces of imbalance. God won't give one electron of energy to sustain the negativity on Earth, so the only way this realm exists is by living parasitically off of our misqualified energy, our negative thoughts and feelings. For centuries these vortexes of accumulated negativity would serve as batteries to energize the forces of imbalance.

On May 8, 1989, through the unified efforts of Heaven and Earth, Violet Lightning from the Heart of God was projected into the pockets of negativity throughout the entire Planet. These bolts of Violet Transmuting Lightning shattered and transmuted the vortexes of negativity, thus sealing them forever in a forcefield of mercy, compassion and forgiveness. This accomplished effectively the goal of Heaven, and "the door where evil dwells" was permanently sealed.

Needless to say, this created havoc in the psychic-astral realm where the forces of imbalance abide. Pandemonium ensued, and these forces became rampant on Earth looking for other avenues to feed and energize their lifeforms. This was the time we were warned about in St. John's Revelation when he stated that in the latter days "Satan would be loosed on Earth."

Because of the presence of the illumined souls on Earth and their increased cooperation with the Heavenly Realms, a plea for assistance was made to Universal Law. An evaluation by God determined that we had progressed sufficiently to allow additional grants of energy to help during this Earthly crisis. An unprecedented incident occurred. For the first time ever, in any system of worlds, the Karmic Board allowed the suspension of free will for a few short days. From June 10th, 1989, to the Summer Solstice on June 21, 1989, free will was held in abeyance. During this time, every man, woman and child evolving on Earth, whether in or out of embodiment, in any dimension or state of consciousness, was drawn into the sacred temple on the inner planes known as the Temple of Reverence for all Life. This occurred in our finer bodies while we slept at night, and no one had a choice in this matter because of the suspension of free will.

Once we were in the temple, we were brought before the Karmic Board, and we were shown a panorama of our past. We were clearly shown the error of our ways, the fall, the choices we have made and the end result of those choices. We recognized our responsibility in the Earthly condition, and we were shown what we have volunteered to do to correct our course and assist in the process of planetary transformation. We were then commanded by the Karmic Board to look into the mirror of life and perceive our own Divinity. Not one soul, regardless of the state of depravity it had fallen to, was allowed to deny the Divinity of its true reality. This reflection of our Divinity was seared into the intelligence of our four lower bodies to filter into our conscious minds in future times.

After we were commanded to perceive our Divinity, the Karmic Board revealed to each of us what would be necessary for us to do in order to transmute our past transgression of the Law of Love and Harmony, so we could move forward in the Light with the rest of our Solar System.

For eleven days during the time our free will was suspended, we were bathed in the Divine quality of Eternal Peace while we contemplated our options. As we slept, we were drawn into the Temple of Eternal Peace that pulsates in the etheric realms over Venezuela in South America. During Sunrise on the morning of the Summer Solstice, the Cosmic tone sounded, and each soul was summoned before the Karmic Board to make a choice as to whether or not they were willing to do what was necessary to transmute their past and move into the Light. Through that choice, free will was re-established.

This sacred event clearly reflects the magnitude of God's mercy and compassion. Many souls had been denying their Divinity for thousands of lifetimes. Now with the reflection of our Divinity seared into the consciousness of our four lower bodies, it will be impossible for us to continue to reject it for any length of time. Even though this activity took place at inner levels, and consequently, most people don't consciously remember it, it doesn't matter. The event is powerfully recorded in our etheric records and memories and will surface when we need it the most.

The Spiritual Hierarchy said this unprecedented experiment was successful beyond Their greatest hope. More souls than they dreamed possible have chosen to fulfill their obligations in the remaining time and move into the Light. This means that our work is being accelerated, and our energy is returning faster than ever to be loved free. But, remember, we are never going to be given anything we can't handle, and we have powerful tools to help us.

The souls that chose not to move forward into the Light (and their number is not many) did so because they decided it was too much work to do what was necessary to clear their past in the short time allotted. They will gradually be taken off the Planet through the natural process of death, and when the time is right, they will be reborn in another system of worlds, again in third dimensional frequencies, but in approximately the caveman state of consciousness, so they won't immediately destroy themselves with technology. The caveman state of consciousness is what Humanity fell to during the creation of the veil of negativity that blinded us from our own Divinity.

Many people will wonder whether or not they have chosen to move forward into the Light. I want to assure you that, if you have any conscious desire to do so at all, you definitely made the positive choice before the Karmic Board. There are also millions of people who made the positive choice who may not have any conscious desire at all to move into the Light just yet. We *never* know what Light burns in a crude exterior, so it is very important for us not to try to figure out who has made the positive choice. In actuality, it is none of our business. What we need to do is focus on our commitments and be about the business of our Father-Mother God, transmuting our past and healing this sweet Earth.

This Divine activity of Light sent a calming unguent of Eternal Peace through the chaos of the psychic-astral realm. The forces of imbalance were greatly diminished as many chose to move into the Light. The remaining few continue to perpetuate their mischief, but the effect has been greatly minimized.

ANCHORING THE FORCEFIELD OF
REVERENCE FOR ALL LIFE

From the Realms of Illumined Truth, it was revealed a short time later that another plan was being set into motion to try and awaken within Humanity the understanding that all life is interrelated, and we are truly One. It is known in Higher Realms that, if this awareness really registers in the minds and feelings of Humanity, we will finally function with a reverence for all life.

The Temple of Reverence for all Life pulsates within the forcefield of the Grand Teton Mountains in Wyoming in the United States of America. Several hundred Lightworkers were directed from on High to gather within this forcefield during the Autumn Equinox on September 23, 1989, to offer themselves as a Unified Cup through which the Light of Reverence for all Life could pour into the physical plane on Earth.

In order for this plan to be as effective as it was hoped it would be by the Heavenly Realms, it was necessary to draw the attention of as many people on the Planet as possible to the Grand Tetons. The Law is "where your attention is, there you are."

The Divine prompting poured forth from the Mind of God into the hearts of the right people, and it was decided in the outer world that a Peace Summit would be held during the week of the Autumn Equinox in the Grant Tetons between Secretary of State James Baker of the United States and Secretary of State Edward Shevardnadze of the Soviet Union. For an entire week, the world turned their attention to this forcefield of Reverence for all Life. Every time anyone saw a television news report of the Peace Summit or read a newspaper article about the progress of the meetings taking place in the Grand Tetons, their energies were woven into the unified chalice of Humanity that was forming within that Sacred Forcefield.

On the dawn of the Autumn Equinox, the Cosmic Tone sounded, and the greatest influx of the Light of Reverence for all Life ever manifest in the world of form poured into the Chalice of Humanity's unified consciousness. This Divine Light of Oneness literally shook the ethers and broke down the barriers of separation. In a few short weeks, on November 9, 1989, we experienced the most dramatic physical manifestations of this fact as we witnessed the crumbling of the Berlin Wall and the initial impulse of the fall of communism.

TIME WARP

With the completion of the anchoring of the frequencies of Oneness and Reverence for all Life, we moved forward into a new opportunity. During November 17, 18 and 19, 1989, a unique phenomenon occurred known as Time Warp.

Time Warp was described by the Spiritual Hierarchy as a dimensional collapsing of time in which the Earth shifted into an accelerated time flow in preparation for moving into the higher frequencies of the Fourth Dimension. This shift actually accelerated our time frequency from a 24-hour day to a 22-hour day. All frequency impulses increased simultaneously, including our clocks, so from outer appearances, it looks like we still have a 24-hour day, but I don't know a single person who hasn't commented about how fast time is flying by.

As a result of this acceleration of time, what we hold in our consciousness and feelings is now manifesting faster. Things seem to be reflecting in our daily lives almost instantly.

A NEW DECADE
NEW OPPORTUNITIES–NEW CHALLENGES

With the God Victorious completion of 1989, we moved into the 1990's more aligned in opportunity and promise than ever before. A global activity known as Campaign for the Earth was born, and the 1990's were heralded as the decade of permanent tangible change.

On April 22, 1990, we celebrated the 20th anniversary of Earth Day, and hundreds of millions of people throughout the globe consented to the healing of Beloved Mother Earth as they awakened to their purpose and reason for being.

DESERT STORM

In the midst of all the joy and expectancy, however, there was a cloud forming on the horizon. It was determined by the Legions of Light that the Earth was in danger, and superhuman assistance was necessary. Prophecy had always indicated that in the latter days there would be a purging that would take place through the Holy Land to transmute the abuse of our Masculine Polarity of Power and the suppression of the Feminine Polarity of Divine Love that is symbolically being acted out by the lifestreams abiding in that area.

When the Nostradamus prophecies of approximately 500 years ago were made, it was revealed that, if Humanity continued our existing course of direction, the purging that would take place in the 1990's in the Holy Land would be so severe that a holocaust nuclear war would occur and the near annihilation of Humanity and the Earth would be the result. At that time, additional Divine dispensations were made to try and avert such a cataclysmic event. More Divine Beings were given permission to embody on Earth, and several contingency plans were prepared to be easily implemented in case the need arose. With the invasion of Kuwait by Iraq on August 2, 1990, the need arose.

ANCHORING THE HIGHWAY OF LIGHT

Lightworkers were asked to gather in the sacred forcefield of Healing through Transmutation and Music that pulsates in the Southwestern United States within the powerful mountain ranges surrounding Tucson, Arizona. This conclave took place over the anniversary of Harmonic Convergence, August 15, 16, 17, 1990. At that time, through the unified consciousness of the Lightworkers gathered there, a Highway of Light was projected from the Heart of the Great Central Sun and anchored into the center of the Earth. This Highway created an open portal through the veil of illusion surrounding the Planet, and it extends several thousand miles in every direction. The Highway of Light is allowing frequencies of the twelve Solar Aspects of Deity to enter the physical plane as never before. This Divine Light is intensifying the planetary forcefield of protection and security that resonates throughout the crystal grid system on Earth, thus embracing this Planet and all her life in an invincible forcefield of protection.

To enable you to experience the magnitude of this Divine Gift, I would like to share with you the words of our Beloved God Parents given through radiation, vibration and consciousness during that cosmic moment:

"Beloved children of the All Encompassing Presence of the Father-Mother God...

"I come to you this sacred day as the White Fire Being of Helios and Vesta, embraced in the White Fire Being of Alpha and Omega, embraced in the White Fire Being of Eloha and Elohae, embraced in the White Fire Being of the Cosmic Presence of God, "I AM" That "I AM".

"Joining with us now in the atmosphere of Earth is the entire Company of Heaven: Crowns; Thrones; Principalities; Galactic Beings; Cosmic Beings; Archangels; Seraphim; Angels; Cherubim; Ascended Masters; the Mighty "I AM" Presences of all Humanity and the Holy Christ Selves; Directors of the Five Elements; Deva Rajas; Devas; Gnomes; Salamanders; Undines and Sylphs.

"Dear Ones, this is an event of Cosmic significance that We in Heaven's Realms have been preparing for for aeons of time. It is critical that you understand the magnitude of this moment, for it is signalling the shift, at an atomic, cellular level, from your downward spiral into oblivion to your ASCENT INTO DIVINITY.

"Ages ago, the clarion call for assistance rang forth from the Heart of Beloved Mother Earth. You, Blessed Ones, responded to her heartfelt plea. You have come from Galaxies beyond Galaxies and Suns beyond Suns in an act of selfless, compassionate service. Time and again, you volunteered to embody on Earth, immersing yourself in the humanly created sea of negativity smothering this blessed Planet. And time and again, through lives of pain and toil, you struggled to create a pinpoint of Light through the psychic-astral plane that would allow the Light of God from the Realms of Perfection to once again shine on Earth. Your success has been limited, and your progress has been ever so slow. But, you continued undaunted by the discouraging appearances of the outer world, clinging tenaciously to the Immaculate Concept for Planet Earth which was revealed to you by your Father-Mother God and encoded in the cellular memory of every fiber of your beings.

"Now, My Beloved Ones, it is time for you to reap the fruits of your labor. Inch by inch, slowly and painfully, you have held the cup of your consciousness aloft, creating an open portal through which the Light of God that is Eternally Victorious could enter the third dimensional plane of Earth. Now, after centuries of time, the Light on Planet Earth has increased sufficiently to allow the Divine Intervention that will transform this sweet Planet and return her and all life evolving upon her to the original Divine Plan re-establishing the etheric blueprint of Heaven on Earth.

"This is a day of God's Victory. It is the third anniversary of Harmonic Convergence, that moment in time when the Feminine Polarity of God's Divine Love was returned to perfect balance with the Masculine Polarity of God's Divine Will in the Realms of Cause, thus enabling the birth of the pure Christ Light of Illumination, Wisdom and Understanding to occur on Earth.

"That pure God Light has been building in momentum daily and hourly the maximum that Cosmic Law will allow. Over the past three years, you have witnessed the awakening taking place within the hearts of Humanity at an accelerated pace. You have also witnessed the extreme imbalances taking place as the frequencies of discord are pushed to the surface in your individual lives and on a global scale as well, so they can be transmuted into Light in preparation for the Earth's ascent into the Fourth Dimension.

"This dual activity of increased Light and accelerated purification has been excruciatingly painful for the masses of Humanity. Many are not able to perceive clearly the opportunity at hand. They attach, through the power of their attention, to the negativity surfacing in their lives, and they amplify it through fear and panic. Consequently, more negativity is created, and the humanly created discord of poverty, disease, war, hate, failure, pollution and fear appears from their limited perception to be overwhelming.

"Humanity, HEAR MY WORDS!

"From the Realms of Perfection, a Cosmic Fiat is ringing

through the Universe.

"FROM THIS DAY FORWARD, ONLY THE LIGHT OF GOD SHALL REIGN VICTORIOUSLY ON EARTH.

"FROM THIS DAY FORWARD, THE RESIDUE OF HU-MANITY'S MISQUALIFIED GIFT OF LIFE SHALL CEASE TO BLIND A SINGLE PARTICLE OF LIFE FROM RECOG-NIZING ITS OWN DIVINITY.

"FROM THIS DAY FORWARD, A TREMENDOUS HIGHWAY OF LIGHT, EXTENDING FROM THE CEN-TRAL MATRIX OF THE SACRED MOUNTAINS SUR-ROUNDING TUCSON, ARIZONA, FOR SEVERAL THOUSAND MILES IN EVERY DIRECTION, WILL BE AN-CHORED FROM THE REALMS OF PERFECTION INTO THE CENTER OF THE EARTH.

"Humanity, HEAR MY WORDS! Can you grasp with your finite minds, Dear Hearts, what this will mean to your evolutionary progress. For millions upon millions of years, the Realms of Perfection have been veiled from your con-scious minds by the psychic-astral sea of chaos surrounding the Planet. On this sacred day, due to the unified efforts of millions of illumined souls over aeons of time, a Highway of Light is being anchored through this sea of negativity that will open a readily accessible pathway for all life on Earth into the Realms of Illumined Truth. Every man, woman and child evolving on Earth, every Elemental and every Angel will NOW be able to easily perceive their own individual God re-ality, their Divine Plan and their purpose and reason for being.

"As above, so below will now become a manifest reality, and the Earth will begin to express her true nature as a Radiant Being of Light.

"Beloved Spirit Sparks, as each of you prepare now to par-ticipate in this Divine Ceremony of Cosmic significance, feel the love of the entire Company of Heaven as We each em-brace you in love and gratitude for your selfless service to the Light.

"All is in readiness. Your opportunity is at hand. BE HERE NOW!"

After the Highway of Light was anchored, another contingency plan was implemented to try and diffuse the disaster forming in the Holy Land.

TRANSMUTING THE ABUSE OF POWER

Again Lightworkers were asked to gather within a sacred forcefield on the Planet. This time the forcefield was in Sun River, Oregon, within the "ring of fire" that connects the volcanic activity of the Pacific Ocean. Since the original abuse of the power center of the throat and the suppression of the heart center of Divine Love began on the continent of Lemuria, the plan was for the Lightworkers to invoke the Violet Fire and transmute the etheric records and memories of the abuse of power back through the ages of time to the original fall, thus dissipating the negativity subconsciously feeding the situation in the Middle East.

On October 17, 1990, the Legions of Light from the entire forcefield of the New Age of Aquarius and the Seventh Solar Aspect of Deity descended into the atmosphere of Earth to assist in magnetizing, from the Heart of God, the Violet Light of Forgiveness, Mercy, Compassion, Transmutation and Freedom. This Light was projected into the mass consciousness of Humanity transmuting cause, core, effect, record and memory, the misqualified thoughts, feelings and actions reflecting our abuse of power back to the beginning of time. The effect of this purification surpassed even the greatest hope of Heaven. The subconscious blocks and resistance to balancing our use of power with Divine Love were thrown asunder. The energy that had sustained the misqualified use of power through aggression, dominance, corruption, manipulation and deception was dissipated. This created a sense of vulnerability and fear that shattered the confidence of those in the world who were wielding their power without the Grace of Divine Love.

On January 16, 1991, the physical purging that was prophesied for the Holy Land began. On the eve of Desert Storm, during the new moon Solar Eclipse, the Light of God poured into the Middle East, embracing the area in a forcefield of protection. Legions of Angels took their strategic positions, standing shoulder to shoulder, as they surrounded the war zone. Through the invocation and prayers of Lightworkers throughout the Planet and the cooperative efforts of Heaven and Earth, the holocaust nuclear war that Nostradamus predicted was averted.

The purging of the imbalance of power occurred with a miraculously minimal loss of life. Every soul is precious, and any loss of life is tragic, but compared to what might have happened, we have the right to be very, very grateful.

ANCHORING THE IMMACULATE HEART
FOR DIVINE GOVERNMENT

With the records and memories of the abuse of power transmuted, our Father-Mother God could now reflect the balance of Divine Love from the Realms of Cause into the physical plane of Earth more effectively. Upon the completion of Desert Storm, it was determined by the Heavenly Realms that the need of the hour on Earth was to re-establish the correct pattern for Divine Government. Needless to say, the governments of the world are responsible for most effectively demonstrating the abuse of power, and in order for Humanity to successfully shift from a consciousness of dominance and aggression to a consciousness of reverence for all life, major changes in our behavior patterns are necessary. Through the window of opportunity that is now open in this dawning New Age, our Father-Mother God began projecting spiritual currents of energy into the atmosphere of Earth to implement a new plan to re-establish the pattern for Divine Government.

This experiment was tried several centuries ago, but unfortunately, the plan failed. Five hundred years ago, Christopher Columbus embarked on a mission to prove the world was round. He was responding to his inner heart call and was being guided by the Realms of Illumined Truth. He was known in inner levels as a Son of Freedom, and he volunteered to assist in "discovering" the new world in which the original experiment for Divine Government would be attempted. His flotilla was first magnetized to the Caribbean Islands. This was not just a coincidence. Pulsating in the etheric realms over these islands is a tremendous vortex of the Violet Flame of Freedom. Columbus connected with this Divine Light, and a powerful Ray of Freedom was anchored in his heart to be carried to the landed surface that would one day form the United States of America.

The word America is an anagram for the I AM RACE. This magnificent country was destined to be the example of Divine Government to all the world. The native American Indians were aware of this Divine Plan. For centuries they had prepared for the coming of a race of God conscious souls. They prepared this land and the nature kingdom through sacred ceremonies and prayer. When the Flame of Freedom was anchored here through Christopher Columbus, they accepted the responsibility of being "keepers of the Flame," and they nurtured and sustained this Sacred Violet Fire of Freedom.

When Christopher Columbus returned to his homeland with the news of the discovery of the new world, the call for freedom reverberated through the Heart Flames of all the oppressed people of the world, and they began to respond.

The original Divine Plan was that the new world of America would be the example to all the world of what Divine Government really is. Contrary to some of the misinformation and the disinformation now being buffeted about, Divine Government does not mean "one world government." Divine Government means each nation governing itself according to the highest good of its people with mutual respect and tolerance for every other government, every nation working together for the highest good of all.

America was to be the home of the "I AM" Race. This was to be a race of God conscious souls aligned with their true God reality, their "I AM" Presence, a race comprised of every race, every nationality, every religion, every creed or doctrine and every philosophy. They were to be self-governed souls working together in perfect harmony and balance, always embracing their use of power with Divine Love and expressing respect, love and tolerance for each other as they valued all life on Earth.

People throughout the world began to respond to their heart's call for freedom—freedom from oppression, domination, aggression and violence, freedom to worship as their inner beings directed. They began to flock to America. Our founding fathers came, and they listened to their inner voice as the Constitution of the United States of America and the Bill of Rights were formulated to align with the Divine Plan for America.

But alas, as has happened time and again throughout the Earth's evolution, the Divine Plan went awry. Human ego, greed, selfishness and the abuse of power took control, and the rest is a sad documentation of history.

Now with the peril of Desert Storm behind us, with the awakening taking place on Earth and with the victory of the opening of the Highway of Light, once again we were called from "above" to anchor the Divine Blueprint for this country in order to correct her course and restore her global mission.

The first step in forming the physical vehicle for any manifest form is the creation of the Immaculate Heart. This is the chalice that will hold the Divine Spark—the Immortal Victorious Three-fold Flame that contains within Its frequencies the Immaculate Concept of the particular Divine Plan involved.

Since Washington, D.C., is considered the seat of government in this country, it was necessary that the Immaculate Heart of Divine Government be anchored within that forcefield.

At inner levels, during our time frame known as the mystical month of May, some very sacred activities take place. The Heavenly Temple known as the Temple of the Immaculate Heart is opened, and all lifestreams preparing to embody in the next twelve month cycle are drawn into that temple. There the purest electrons from their beings are magnetized to form their Immaculate Heart, the chalice that will hold their Three-fold Flame while they are in embodiment on Earth.

In May of 1991, the purest electrons available were drawn to form the forcefield of the Immaculate Heart for Divine Government which was to be anchored in Washington, D.C. Again the focused attention of Humanity was critical in order to create a unified chalice of consciousness through which the Immaculate Heart would manifest into the physical plane. Remember, where your attention is, there you are. In order to draw the attention of the world to Washington, D.C., and to focus the attention of Humanity on the heart, Divine Intervention was necessary. The first weekend in May the Light of God poured into the Planet, and the appearance of a slight irregular heartbeat temporarily manifested in President Bush. This event drew the attention of the entire world to the "heart of government" in Washington, D.C., in a way that nothing else could have. Through this activity, God's Victory was assured, and the Immaculate Heart of Divine Government was anchored in perfect order.

THE CONJUNCTION OF VENUS, MARS AND JUPITER

Now all was in readiness for the next step of the Divine Plan of planetary transformation. This step involved a Cosmic push to expand the Feminine Polarity of Divine Love from the inner Realms of Cause into the physical plane of Earth. It occurred through a rare astronomical alignment.

In June, 1991, the almost perfect conjunction of the planets

Venus, Mars and Jupiter occurred. Spiritually, Venus always represents the Feminine Polarity of Divine Love. Mars represents the Masculine Polarity of Power, and Jupiter represents expansion and growth of spiritual freedom. All of these planets were joined together in the forcefield of the constellation of Leo on June 18, 1991, which was the moment of closest conjunction. Leo represents Solar energy at its most powerful frequency and love in its purest form. The radiance from this celestial formation bathed the Earth for several days in the balanced expansion of Divine Power and Divine Love, the pure essence of our Father-Mother God. This influx of Divine Light assisted in breaking down the patterns of resistance that were keeping people stuck in dysfunctional, oppressive situations which were preventing them from releasing and letting go of people, places, conditions or things that were no longer serving their highest good.

The crystallized negativity that had kept Humanity stuck in old destructive patterns and belief systems of the past began to melt and take on a more fluid and flexible form. The molecules of discord began to float apart, and the balanced Light of our Father-Mother God began to interpenetrate the dense forcefields of negativity for the first time in aeons.

THE SOLAR ECLIPSE

With the Light of God blazing in, through and around every electron of precious life energy evolving on Earth, we were now ready for a Cosmic experiment. This was an experiment that had never before been tried in any system of worlds, an experiment of unprecedented Divine Intervention. Every illumined soul in embodiment on Earth was prepared at inner levels while they slept at night to assist in the plan. We were each given an opportunity to renew our vows to love all life on Earth free, which we had taken within the Heart of God before this embodiment. A new level of purpose and commitment began to filter into our conscious minds, and we began to intuitively perceive the urgency of the hour.

To assist in the experiment, Legions of Cosmic and Ascended Beings from the entire Universe descended into the atmosphere of Earth and took Their strategic positions around the Planet to embrace this sweet Earth in an invincible forcefield of love and protection.

The experiment took place during a rare celestial alignment of the Sun, the Moon and the Earth, a unique Solar Eclipse that was held in the momentum of the new moon. Solar Eclipses occur fairly regularly on the Planet, approximately two per year, but the eclipse that took place on July 11, 1991, was rare in that it was a full seven minutes of total alignment, the longest an eclipse ever lasts. This unusual Solar Eclipse was held in the embrace of two full moon Lunar Eclipses, one on June 26, 1991, and one on July 26, 1991.

During the seven minutes of perfect alignment of the Solar Eclipse, all of the pressures of imbalance, discord and karma were temporarily lifted from every cell, atom, electron and sub-atomic particle on the physical realm of Earth. During that Cosmic Moment, the only forces in action on the physical plane were the Fire Pillars of Love and Power of our Father-Mother God, blending in perfect balance, realigning the foundations of consciousness on Earth with Divinity. The central core of perfection that continues to beat within the heart of every electron of life existing on Earth was activated.

The Solar Impulse of our Father-Mother God arced out of the Great Central Sun entering the physical Plane of Earth completely unopposed and unimpeded. The power of this sacred Light accelerated the core of perfection within EVERY atom. This profoundly affected the substance of organic/ cellular life on Earth, particularly in the DNA and RNA in which the blueprint for the Planet's Divine Plan is recorded. This substance contains the plan of absolute perfection on the physical realm.

During the moment of the Solar Eclipse, our God Parents released a Violet Ray of Freedom that was the perfect balance of the Masculine Polarity of Divine Power–Sapphire Blue and the Feminine Polarity of Divine Love–Pink. The Violet Ray of Freedom, which was able to enter the Earth for the very first time unimpeded by negativity, TRANSMUTED INTO FOURTH DIMENSIONAL FREQUENCIES OF PERFECTION, 50 PERCENT OF ALL OF THE ENERGY THAT HAS EVER BEEN MISQUALIFIED ON EARTH. This energy was transmuted mostly from unconscious and subconscious realms. This literally means that 50% of every electron of precious life energy we have ever misqualified in any existence or dimension, both known and unknown, through the misuse of our creative faculties of thought and feeling, IS GONE!!!

This negative energy has interpenetrated our beings at a cellular level for aeons of time holding sway over our atomic vehicles. This is why disease and distress seem so prevalent in our human experience. With this purification, a re-alignment and re-balancing has occurred at a deep atomic level. Now the Solar Healing of our God Parents will profoundly affect the living cells of Humanity and the Nature Kingdom as well as the molecules, atoms, electrons and sub-atomic particles of all life within Earth's realms (animate and inanimate). This will accelerate the physics, chemistry and biology of life on Earth into Fourth Dimensional consciousness. In simple words, this transmutation of negativity scientifically assures the Ascension of this Planet HERE and NOW! The effects of this cause will now allow each of us to more quickly rediscover our own Divine Plan, free from ONE HALF of the old baggage from our past.

THE SOLAR INBREATH

With 50% of the mass karma of Humanity and the other lifewaves on Earth transmuted, a door of opportunity opened during the eclipse to allow even greater assistance from on High. The purification of 50% of our past ensured the inclusion of the physical realm of Earth in a Solar Inbreath that involved our entire Solar System. A Solar Inbreath is a multi-dimensional activity of Light in which our Father-Mother God breathe all life closer to Their own Divine Three-fold Flame. This activity aligns all of the Three-fold Flames that pulsate in any part of life. The Three-fold Flame at any point of evolution is the focal point of unity with the whole of creation. Even though all parts of life evolve in different directions with different goals and different experiences, at certain points in each great Cosmic Cycle, all activity is suspended "for a Cosmic moment" to reconfirm that all life is ONE... and that this fundamental condition of the Universe remains primary and absolute! This is termed a Solar Inbreath.

The Solar Inbreath connotates a movement in toward the center. When we breathe, we breathe in toward our Heart Flame, and so do our God Parents. But this Solar Inbreath occurred not in the physical realm as measured by distance or time. Rather, it occurred in the Realms of Consciousness where an alignment of all Three-fold Flames brought an accelerated magnetic cohesion amongst all the component parts. This reconfirmed that God's First Cause of Perfection for all life has complete dominion throughout the whole of creation. This is symbolized in physical terms as if the Planets are drawn closer to the Sun. What does occur for all Planets is a more perfect orbital pattern and accelerated core planetary vibration through the planetary Three-fold Flame. In the Earth's case, it also included a gentle, but sure, straightening of the planetary axis.

During the Solar Inbreath, the alignment of all Three-fold Flames was not just vertical (between the various realms and dimensions of this Universe) but also horizontal (within each realm and dimension). This is particularly true for the physical realm of Humanity. A certain fundamental alignment of all Three-fold Flames within Humanity was produced so "the whole of Humanity," through its center, can rise into the Fourth Sphere of Unconditional Divine Love. This opportunity ended all separateness permanently... not only of Earth and Humanity from the Divinity of the Universe, but it also ended the separation of Humanity from the influence of our own Three-fold Flame of Cosmic Balance and Healing. Remember, the Three-fold Flame at the center of every human being is the same Flame in the Central Sun.

At the moment of the Solar Eclipse, and sustained thereafter, the Three-fold Flame of every human being (in and out of embodiment) was fundamentally changed, completely aligned with and further empowered by the Three-fold Flame of Alpha and Omega from the Central Sun. This will allow each Three-fold Flame to now function like the Sun Itself and begin an Inbreath of all the energies of the four lower vehicles of each individual into the Sun or Christ Self... gradually, but very assuredly, raising all the energy and vibration of that lifestream into Fourth Dimensional Consciousness.

The Three-fold Flame was to be the Source of all guidance and development of the Universe, including our own sphere of influence on Earth. In the history of Humanity's evolution, the source of guidance and authority shifted to the human ego, bringing about the present difficult and painful experiences now related to physical embodiment. However, there shall now be a fundamental shift back to the Three-fold Flame as the Source of all guidance and authority for Humanity's development. The Solar Eclipse/Inbreath was God's mark of this shift.

THE STRAIGHTENING OF THE AXIS

Along with the Inbreath, a gentle straightening of our planetary axis occurred during the Solar Eclipse.

The axis around which an individual or Planet develops determines the realms of experience open to that being. If an axis is bent (out of alignment in consciousness more so than physically), access to other realms becomes difficult and ofttimes distorted, hence, Humanity's individual and collective difficulty in achieving higher consciousness and, unfortunately, the tendency toward opening to the distorted realms of psychic and astral chaos. We can see why the axis of Earth must be straight and aligned with the Solar Axis. The "Sceptre of Power," which an axis represents, determines the "orbit" and how far a being might reach out in his/her evolving God Consciousness. Every evolving individual, Planet or Sun, has a spine/axis around which it evolves, which determines its experience. The Cosmic Inbreath, at the moment of the Solar Eclipse on July 11, 1991, brought the greatest straightening of Earth's axis yet known, aligning her with the perfect axis and "Orbit of Consciousness" she was always intended to have as an evolving Planet. This quickened her core vibration, accelerating the masses toward Christ Consciousness and the Lightworkers toward Solar Consciousness.

WHAT IS THE EFFECT OF THE SOLAR ECLIPSE

With the success of the Solar Eclipse, we have entered a new period of time (...or timelessness) with distinct new potentialities/realities for life as it exists on Earth. The science of physics will tell us that all particles of life answer to the center, to the primary forces within the Universe. These primary forces are embodied in the Solar Three-fold Flame within the Sun and the Twelve-fold Aspect of Deity radiating out from the Sun. This Solar Radiation shall more profoundly affect Humanity now because of the expansion of our Three-fold Flame. If we think of life in scientific terms and know that we are but a particle of Light, as is the Earth, we will begin to understand with greater clarity the truth of our being. All particles of Light answer the call from the center and align perfectly along the Central Axis of Love, Wisdom, and Power of this Universe. This means that, according to our acceptance of our Solar Identity on the physical plane, our time for living in Heaven on Earth has now arrived.

I know this sounds truly wonderful, and it is, but you may be asking "If this is true, why are we still feeling the way we do?" In my counseling, I have patients telling me they are waking up grieving in the morning with nothing going on in their lives to justify such sadness. Others are having anxiety attacks; others (both men and women) feel like they have terminal P.M.S. People are feeling empty, lost, isolated, abandoned, afraid and disoriented. Some feel like they have "holes in their auras" or like part of them is missing. People are confused and baffled.

I want to assure you that even though this is uncomfortable, it is perfectly natural. After all, 50% of everything we have identified with since the "fall of man" is gone. Even though these patterns and beliefs made us miserable, they were all we knew. They were familiar. It is the equivalent of an abused child who fights tooth and nail not to be taken away from his abusive parents. Even though the child may be in a life threatening, painful situation, he doesn't know the difference, and the fear of the unknown is worse than leaving his parents. That is what is happening to Humanity now. Half of the negative patterns that have been part of us for aeons of time are now gone, and we feel a sense of loss. That explains the grieving, the fear and the emptiness. We are grieving the loss of part of ourselves, but what we must keep in mind is that this is *only* the part that reflects pain, poverty, disease, hate, anger, failure, war, unworthiness, low self-esteem and all other misqualified patterns now existing on Earth. This means the wonderful patterns that enhance our ability to create joy and success in every facet of our existence are now much more accessible.

Once the abused child adjusts to the new family environment and feels what it is like to be nurtured, valued and loved, he would never choose voluntarily to return to the abusive situation. Neither will we. It's just that we need to allow ourselves time to adjust to the new frequencies. There are several things that will help:

1. Flood your four lower bodies and your environment with the pink essence of Divine Love every day. This will fill

the void where the negativity used to be and heal the feeling of loss.

2. Be cognizant of the fact that every single challenge that presents itself to you from now on is just part of the remaining 50% coming up to be transmuted. Detach from it emotionally and handle it objectively, knowing that as each situation is handled harmoniously and effectively with the Violet Fire of Freedom, your percentage of negativity is diminishing. Soon it will ALL be gone.

3. Focus on the Light! Darkness cannot be sustained in the presence of Light. What you put your attention on is amplified, so amplify only the good. Energize with your thoughts and feelings the vision of your transformation. See yourself healthy, happy, prosperous, deeply loved, fulfilled, unlimited and FREE.

4. To assist during this critical time of transition, a Violet Fire Angel has volunteered to remain in the aura of every man, woman and child on the Planet. These legions of Angels have made a compassionate sacrifice and will help us to transmute the energy we may misqualify each day. Focus on this selfless friend in your energy field and ask him/her to help you adjust to your new-found freedom.

5. Participate in the global opportunities to anchor Light on Earth.

RE-DEDICATING THE PLANET EARTH TO THE LIGHT

After the victory of the Solar Eclipse, the Earth was ready for re-dedication to the Light.

There are energy vectors throughout the Planet known as stargates. Originally, prior to the fall of man, the stargates were open conduits over which the Light from the Solar Aspect of Deity of the prevailing constellation for the Age was channeled into the third dimensional frequencies of Earth.

This greatly assisted evolving Humanity. It enabled the Divine Qualities of the current Age to bathe the vehicles of all life on Earth, and it allowed Humanity to learn to quickly utilize the gifts, knowledge, wisdom and Light of that particular Solar Aspect of Deity. This enhanced our growth and immensely accelerated our progress.

Unfortunately, when Humanity started misqualifying energy and the psychic-astral sea of negativity began forming around the Planet, some of our discord filtered out through the open conduits of the stargates and contaminated other areas of our Solar System. This was a crisis that had to be stopped, and the only solution seemed to be closing the stargates. This action was decreed by Cosmic Law, and in one mighty stroke, the stargates were closed, and the Earth was sealed off from the rest of the Solar System in a forced quarantine. This was indeed a tragedy of Cosmic proportions.

For millions of years, Humanity has struggled without the benefit of the open stargates, and consequently, our progress has been painfully slow. Now, with the urgency of the hour upon us and hundreds of thousands of illumined souls embodied on the Planet, a plan was set into motion to see if Humanity could be raised in consciousness sufficiently to allow the stargates for Aquarius to be opened without affecting the rest of our Solar System adversely.

When the stargates for an Age are opened, the "keeper of the gates" is the opposite constellation in the natural zodiac. The "keeper of the stargates" for the Age of Aquarius is the constellation of Leo.

The Light of the Seventh Solar Aspect of Deity which emanates through the forcefield of Aquarius originally entered the physical plane of Earth through the stargate known as the Lion's Gate. (The lion is the symbol of Leo.) The Lion's Gate is the energy vector in the etheric realms over Giza, Egypt. Some 10,000 years ago, during the Age of Leo, the great Sphinx was built in preparation for the day when the Lion's Gate would again be opened.

In August of the year 1951 during the astrological sign of Leo, a plan was set into motion by the Spiritual Hierarchy to prepare for the opening of the Lion's Gate which would enable the spiritual energies of Aquarius to once again flow into Earth unimpeded by human consciousness.

The project began by our Father-Mother God sending forth spiritual currents of energy from the Great Central Sun, thus initiating a forty year "trial" period for the Earth. Forty has always been considered the mystical number of initiation. It represents four increments of ten. Each of these four increments symbolizes one of our four lower bodies and one of the four elements: physical/earth, etheric/air, mental/fire, emotional/water. It is by becoming master of our four lower bodies that our Ascension is realized. In the last Age, the number forty was mentioned several times in reference to great initiations. The purging flood of Noah lasted forty days. Jesus fasted for forty days and forty nights before his final initiation into Christhood. After the resurrection, Jesus prepared for forty days for His Ascension. In the great mystery schools, forty days of preparation is necessary for any major initiation.

Since August of 1951, the Earth has been in the process of mass initiation. For four increments of ten years each, the Spiritual Hierarchy has been initiating the four lower bodies and the four elements of Earth into higher octaves of Light in preparation for the opening of the Lion's Gate. In retrospect, we can observe the Cosmic push. We have undergone a drastic ecological, sociological and technological revolution in a very short period of time. We have been struggling to balance the essence of the four elements in preparation for the shift in frequency of vibration.

With the God Victorious accomplishments of the past few years, our initiations were complete. On August 8, 1991 (8:8), the Lion's Gate was activated. 8 is the universal symbol of infinity, and it fulfills the Divine Law "as above, so below." During that Cosmic activation, the Sphinx fulfilled its mission, and the spiritual Light of the New Age of Aquarius began flooding the Earth.

One of the ancient Tibetan prophecies states "The Golden Age shall begin when the stone lion in the desert stands up and reveals itself."

Remember, Leo is the symbol of pure Solar energies, and the Sphinx is the archetype representing our Solar Vehicles. The advent of the opening of the Lion's Gate brought a significant shift from the influence of our four lower physical vehicles to the influence of the Solar Vehicles of our God Presence.

Through our four lower vehicles, God and our Divinity were perceived with obscurity. This created within us the consciousness of limitation. Now, with the predominant influence of our Solar Presence, we will be able to clearly recognize our Divinity and accept the fact that we are limitless Sons and Daughters of God.

With the activation of the Lion's Gate and the influx of Light from the forcefield of Aquarius, the Planet Earth was officially re-dedicated to the Light. The seven physical chakras along our physical planetary spines were raised up in vibration and were permanently merged with the twelve Solar chakras along the Solar Spine of our God Presence. When this fusing of chakras occurred, every electron of our four lower bodies was activated in preparation for the anchoring of the Divine Blueprint. This activity severed the bonds of limitation that held us in patterns of separation and unworthiness. It broke the codes that programmed us into the belief patterns of duality, such as good and evil, judgment and limitation.

This activation occurred through the spinal column or spiritual axis of every human being evolving on Earth whether in or out of embodiment. It then was reflected into the atomic substance of all physical matter. This activated the cellular structures of all manifest form on Earth, thus preparing every particle of life to receive the Divine Blueprint for the "new Heaven and the new Earth" which was the next step scheduled for this Planet in the transformational process of her rebirth.

ANCHORING THE DIVINE BLUEPRINT

After the opening of the Lion's Gate, the Violet Light of the Seventh Solar Aspect of Deity began pouring into Earth, activating the core of purity in every electron of life, creating a receptive environment for the Divine Blueprint. All was in readiness for the next step of the Divine Plan.

Lightworkers were asked to gather within the forcefield of the Immaculate Heart for Divine Government which had been anchored in Washington, D.C. We were asked to take advantage of the spiritual currents of energy that flow through the Universe during the anniversary of Harmonic Convergence, thus optimizing our humble third dimensional efforts, creating the greatest opportunity for success.

All manifest form begins with a blueprint, and the anchoring of the Divine Blueprint for the "new Heaven and the new Earth" was imperative in order for the upward shift in Humanity's consciousness to be accomplished as ordained by Cosmic Law.

On August 18, 1991, the Divine Blueprint for the transformed Earth in all her glory was anchored into the receptive core of purity in every electron of physical matter. This affected the RNA-DNA patterning of all life. The perfected patterns, which form the matrix for all transformation, are now readily available. This will enable each of us to walk through the challenges surfacing in our lives with less struggle.

The Divine Blueprint now activated in all life will first reflect in the Realms of Cause. Then, we will begin seeing tangible proof of the shift in our everyday lives.

The Divine Blueprint contains within its patterns the frequencies of Divine Government, prosperity, vibrant health, loving relationships, fulfilling jobs, peace, harmony, happiness, joy, freedom and all other positive expressions of life. Now that these patterns are available, we will truly see what it means by the transformation taking place in "the twinkling of an eye."

Within twelve hours after the blueprint for Divine Government was anchored, the coup in the Soviet Union was attempted. This failed attempt struck the final blow to communism and established a momentum of democracy and freedom that will be unstopable.

ACTIVATING THE CRYSTAL AMETHYST GRID SYSTEM

During the Autumn Equinox on September 23, 1991, an evaluation was made from on High to determine if any of Humanity's negativity was contaminating the rest of the Solar System by filtering out through the open stargate in Giza, Egypt. To the relief and joy of the Heavenly Realms, it was not. The Violet Fire Angels Who had been stationed in the auras of all Humanity during the Solar Eclipse, were effectively assisting us in transmuting our daily misqualified energy, and the Lightworkers who invoke the Violet Fire to transmute the remaining mass karma on Earth were also effectively keeping the negativity in check.

The success of this God Victorious accomplishment opened the door for the next step of our planetary transformation. The Lightworkers were asked to gather in the power point of the crystal amethyst grid system in Thunder Bay, Canada. This is the forcefield of the largest amethyst mines in North America. As we reached up into the Realms of Illumined Truth, we were told by the Spiritual Hierarchy that a plan was in motion to amplify the activation of the crystal grid system, restoring it to its Divine Purpose.

The crystal grid system is the electrical system of the Planet. It is Mother Earth's computer and functions exactly like our own bodily electrical system of chakras, energy meridians and acupuncture points. Prior to the "fall of man," this crystal system very effectively received Light from our Father-Mother God and transmitted it into every particle of life, thus energizing and sustaining all physical matter. The stargates that were open to receive the stepped down Solar

Aspect of the prevailing constellation of the Age projected the pure God Light into the crystal grid system, and through this system, the Divine qualities of the Age were amplified through all life.

As long as we were fulfilling the Divine Plan on Earth, this sytem worked perfectly. It merely radiated the Light of God into the physical plane of Earth and amplified everything in its path. Unfortunately, when Humanity began experimenting with our creative faculties of thought and feeling in ways that were conflicting with God's Will, the crystal grid system amplified the negativity as well. As we sank further and further into the depths of chaos, the crystal grid system, which is programmed to amplify everything in its path, became a source of great pain. It was actually adding to the demise of Earth rather than perpetuating life as it was originally intended to do. During that time of great confusion on Earth, it was decided by God, as a merciful activity to life, to withdraw the energy from the crystal grid system and allow only the amount of energy that would sustain physical consciousness to be transmitted through the crystals. This act of compassion eased the amplification of negativity, but tragically, it also reduced the amplification of God's Light. At this point, we truly became the "dark star."

Since that moment in time, the crystal system has been greatly misunderstood and abused. The illumined souls, who were few and far between at that time, knew they were not to utilize the crystal energy because of the pain it caused by amplifying the discord on Earth, but the souls who abused their power learned to use the crystal energy to manipulate and control people. We have all heard of crystal balls and other forms of crystals used by proponents of the dark arts such as the black magicians. The misuse of crystal energy was one of the main causes of the sinking of Atlantis. Because of this, there have been continual warnings in the world religions against using crystals. Even now, some of the religious leaders are equating crystals with "devil worship," but crystals in themselves are neutral, just as the atom is neutral. It is Humanity that chose to utilize atomic energy to form weapons of mass destruction. Fortunately, even through all of the misuse and struggle, the Immaculate Concept for the crystal grid system has been held in the Divine Mind of God in preparation for the time when Humanity would awaken sufficiently to allow it to be restored to its Divine Intent and Purpose. With the rejoicing support of the entire Company of Heaven, THIS IS THE TIME.

An experiment was implemented during Harmonic Convergence in August, 1987, and the crystal grid system received its first level of activation. This began the gentle increase of Light through the electrical system on Earth. We were advised from on High at the time that this would begin a purging process on Earth that would gradually increase for approximately five years. The order of the day during that time frame would be "all that is hidden must now be revealed." Activities of life based in corruption and oppression would begin to crumble and be pushed to the surface for clearing and transformation. All we have to do is observe the catastrophic and monumental changes that have taken place on Earth individually and globally since 1987, and we will recognize the truth of that information. It was reflected to us from the Realms of Truth that, if the experiment was successful, additional assistance would be given by our Father-Mother God to allow the perfect re-activation of the crystal grid system. With the God Victorious accomplishments of the past few years, the experiment was successful even beyond the expectations of Heaven. So, on September 30, 1991, the day celebrated as the Angelic Harvest, the Light of God poured through the unified cup created by all Lightworkers on the Planet (whether they were consciously aware of it or not) and entered the amethyst crystal grid system in Thunder Bay, Canada. The Light was then transmitted through the entire crystal grid system on Earth, and this precious source of Light was once again restored to its original Divine Service.

EARTH'S ORBITAL ADJUSTMENT AND THE OPENING
OF THE REMAINING STARGATES OF AQUARIUS

The victory of this activation allowed additional information to be revealed regarding the next step of the Divine Plan for Earth. We were informed by the Realms of Illumined Truth that the Earth was in great peril, and a critical orbital adjustment was necessary in order to assure safe passage into the Fourth Dimension. It seems that when the Light was withdrawn from the crystal grid system, the frequency of vibration of the atomic and sub-atomic particles of physical matter began to slow down. This created a heaviness and a denseness that actually bent the axis of the Earth and caused her to fall into an orbital pattern many octaves below where she was supposed to be. Historically, the jolt from the "fall" to a denser orbit caused what has been called the "flipping of the poles" and the "instant ice ages" that swept the Earth freezing dinosaurs in their tracks. Some are being discovered in frozen tundra now with the food they were eating still in their mouths.

As a Solar System evolves, it ascends up a spiral of Light from one dimension into another. When the Earth fell out of her correct orbit, she was off track and not in alignment to ascend into the next spiral of the Fourth Dimension. (See chart page 73.) The Legions of Light informed us that in order for Earth to make the planetary move into the Fourth Dimension, we must first ascend back into our correct orbit. The problem with this was that we would again have to cross over the abyss that caused the jolt to Earth and allowed the poles to "flip." The seers and prophets of Ages past saw this peril and consequently, predicted cataclysmic earthquakes and earth changes for these "end times."

Fortunately, everything that could conceivably be done by Heaven and Earth to avert such catastrophe was done.

Since the opening of the first Aquarian Stargate over Giza, Egypt, did not adversely affect the Universe, it was agreed by our Father-Mother God to open the other eleven Stargates of Aquarius. Each of the twelve constellations has twelve stargates, a total of the sacred geometric number of 144. In the original plan during the 2000 year influence of a particular constellation, the twelve stargates for that system were to be opened wider than the others, so that the Divine Gifts of that Solar Aspect of Deity would pour into Earth unimpeded by human consciousness. When the stargates were closed and the Earth was quarantined, the only way the current Aspect of Deity had access to the physical plane was to be drawn through the consciousness of someone in the physical plane. The great problem was, of course, that awakened souls were few and far between, and the purity of the Light was always subject to the consciousness of the person it was passing through. Consequently, very little really pure Light entered the physical plane. The stargates, however, are direct open portals through which the pure Light of the Aspects of Deity can be stepped down into physical frequencies and flood the Earth without having to pass through Humanity's consciousness.

After the activation of the crystal grid system on September 30, 1991, with mighty bolts of Violet Lightning, the other eleven Stargates of Aquarius were opened in the following order:

1. Giza, Egypt–The Lion's Gate (opened 8-8-91)

   The following opened September 30, 1991

2. Thunder Bay, Canada

3. Southwestern United States of America

4. Cuba and the Caribbean Islands

5. Brazil

6. Sumatra–South Pacific

7. New Zealand

8. South Africa

9. Beijing, China

10. St. Petersburg, Soviet Union

11. Arctic–North Pole

12. Antarctic–South Pole

Through this Divine Ceremony, the Seventh Aspect of

Deity from Aquarius began flooding every particle of life. The God qualities of Forgiveness, Freedom, Mercy, Compassion, Transmutation, Liberty, Divine Justice and Opportunity began to penetrate every electron of physical substance on Earth. This created a shift of vibration on the Planet that lifted us up enough to enable us to form a bridge across the abyss into our correct orbit.

The Divine etheric pattern for Earth has always remained in the correct orbit even when Earth fell away. This etheric pattern is a magnetic forcefield that has unsuccessfully been trying to draw the Earth back into her correct orbit for aeons of time. In a Divine Ceremony, the Lightworkers gathered at Thunder Bay, and those joined in consciousness from around the world created a unified Presence which expanded to engulf the entire Planet. The unified body of Group Avatar aligned with the axis of the Earth, and our spinal columns became one with that shaft of Light. Our seven planetary chakras merged with the seven planetary chakras aligned along the axis of the Planet, and as one breath, one heartbeat, one consciousness of Holy Spirit, we projected seven mighty shafts of Violet Light into the axis of the Divine etheric pattern of the New Earth pulsating in the correct orbit. This created a bridge of freedom that built in momentum for several days. Then, in another Divine Ceremony on October 4, 1991, an unparalleled influx of the Ascension Flame poured through the twelve open Stargates of Aquarius, and this sweet Earth ascended in perfect safety over the bridge to freedom into her correct spiral in preparation for her passage through the doorway into the Fourth Dimension.

This prepared us for the beginning of a 20 year process in which the Light of the World will be daily and hourly increasing. We were told by the Realms of Truth during Harmonic Convergence that the move into the Fourth Dimension would be a 25 year span of time beginning on August 17, 1987. The first five years would be the most tumultuous as the purging was accelerated. We would then go through a series of quantum shifts in vibration that would move us through the "doorway" from the third dimension into the Fourth Dimension, and it would take 20 years, until the year

2012, to complete the Ascension into our new spiral.

The quantum shifts I have described to you were victoriously accomplished in 1991. Now, we are ready for our 20 year acceleration. During this time, we will still be going through our learning experiences, but we will have levels of clarity and understanding that we have never experienced before in order to handle our challenges more effectively. This will be a time when the Light of God will be available to assist in expanding the Divine Blueprint for the "new Heaven and the new Earth." This will be a time when the reality of limitless physical perfection can become manifest.

On January 11, 1992, we began the ascent through the doorway that unites the third dimensional spiral with the Fourth Dimensional Spiral.

Functioning in the eternal moment of now, I will discuss this 20 year process. Regardless of when you are reading this book, experience it in present time. This is an active ongoing process, and each time we experience it, we intensify its power and effectiveness.

On the anniversary of this quantum shift in vibration, January 11th of each year until the year 2012, we will be given another opportunity to ascend further into the Octaves of Perfection. Step by step, our transformation will be accomplished until, eventually, all life evolving on this sweet Earth is wholly Ascended and free.

This is a sacred time of unprecedented opportunity in the history of this blessed Planet's evolution. It is a time when our self-inflicted separation from God will be healed, a time when we will reach up into the Realms of Illumined Truth and tap the Wisdom of the Ages. Then, we will truly understand what duality is, and we will learn to bring it into perfect balance.

As is always the case when a major event such as the one at hand begins to filter into the consciousness of Humanity, the various interpretations of what is happening create a sense of confusion and, often, even direct conflict. That is why we must each invoke the Light of discernment and the Flame of Illumined Truth through all we see and hear. We must ask our God Presence to filter out every trace of human consciousness, so we will be able to absorb only the truth that will set us free. I ask that you please do that now before reading the rest of this information.

HUMANLY CREATED DUALITY

Duality is a concept that has been misunderstood since the "fall of man" aeons ago. Due to the abuse of our gift of "free will," the original Divine Plan for Planet Earth has gone far awry. Duality, as we perceive it today, is "good and evil," and yet, this was never part of the original plan on Earth.

The biblical allegory of Adam and Eve symbolically reflects this truth. The Garden of Eden (Earth) was created to sustain human life in the most glorious way possible. Everything that Humanity (Adam and Eve) needed to survive in total harmony was provided by God and the Kingdom of Nature. The gift of free will was given so that Humanity could choose each day how we would use our precious gift of life... How today shall I expand the borders of my Father's Kingdom? How today shall I use my thoughts, words, actions and feelings to add to the Light of the world?

In all that perfection, there was only one admonition given to us by our God Parents and that was WE MUST NOT PARTAKE OF THE TREE OF KNOWLEDGE OF GOOD AND EVIL. But Humanity did "eat the apple" and began experimenting with our gift of life in destructive ways, creating negative thoughtforms that reflected on the environment. This resulted in the eventual "fall of man." Humanity became so immersed in our self-created chaos and pain that we could no longer perceive our Divine Purpose. We continued creating denser and denser vibrations of negativity until we manifested such a chasm between ourselves and our knowledge of God that we felt isolated to struggle in our misery alone.

In order for us to grasp the real meaning of the opportunity at hand, we must understand with greater clarity the meaning of FREE WILL. Free will is a gift that is given to each Lifestream who comes forth from the Heart of God at the moment of creation. This gift is given to enable each of us, through conscious choice, to expand the borders of our Father's Kingdom by becoming masters of our lives, creating perfection in every dimension of our existence. It was never part of the Divine Plan for us to use this gift of free will to create anything other than good. Never was it intended that Humanity would choose to use our gift of life to create chaos, confusion, disease, poverty, war, lack, limitation, fear, hatred and all other forms of grossly misqualified energy that are now manifesting in the world. This discord has become so prevalent on Earth that we have actually deceived ourselves into accepting that it is a natural part of life, and even worse, we attribute it to, of all things, God's Will.

This duality of good and evil has become such an obvious part of our Earthly existence that we have even gone to the extreme of believing that without evil we cannot experience good. This is, by far, the most destructive belief system we could have. Our thoughts are creative, and as long as we believe good cannot exist without evil, we will continually create and perpetuate the negativity now existing on Earth. The reality is the moment has arrived when the Lord's Prayer will be brought to fruition: THY KINGDOM COME, THY WILL BE DONE ON EARTH AS IT IS IN HEAVEN. The frequencies of discord and disintegration now existing on Earth do not exist in the Octaves of Light. Nothing less than Perfection–God's Will–manifests in the Heavenly Realms, and that is the Divine Heritage of Earth.

Evil, as we know it, is a human creation. God will not give one electron of precious life energy to sustain the negativity existing on Earth. This dimension lives parasitically off of Humanity's misqualified energy. It is impossible for the discordant frequencies of evil (disease, war, hate, poverty, anger and on ad infinitum) to move forward into the Fourth Dimensional Octaves of Light. The only way evil can move through the doorway into the Octaves of Light is by being transmuted back into its original perfection *first*. The lifestreams sustaining evil, often referred to as the sinister force or the lords of darkness, must also choose to move into the Light in order to pass through the doorway into the Fourth Dimension.

Because of God's infinite compassion, those refusing to move forward into the Light will be given the opportunity to progress on another Planet at a slower pace.

The Universal Law of... "as 'I Am' lifted up, all life is lifted up with me," must now be the continual affirmation upon our lips during this Cosmic Moment. It is critical that we do not focus on "evil or darkness" at this time, but rather that we turn the full power of our attention to the Light and become the greatest force of Light we are capable of being. Darkness cannot be sustained in the presence of Light. This is both a physical and a spiritual Law. Healing our self-inflicted separation is not unifying and merging "good and evil." It is balancing the polarities of God within our beings.

THE TRUE MEANING OF DUALITY

Duality, as originally reflected on Earth, was and is the Polarity of Divinity which is the MASCULINE (Power) and FEMININE (Love) Aspects of God, not good and evil.

As mentioned previously, the Masculine Polarity of God is Divine Power and reverberates through the throat center on a frequency of Sapphire Blue Light. It activates the left brain hemisphere, the rational, logical mind. The Feminine Polarity of God is Divine Love and reverberates through the heart center on a frequency of Pink Light. It activates the right brain hemisphere, the creative, intuitive mind.

When these two polarities are vibrating in perfect balance, they awaken within the brain the centers of the Sunshine Yellow Light of Enlightenment and Wisdom. This activity is known to many as attaining Christ Consciousness, and through this process, the Crown Chakra of Illumination is opened.

The self-inflicted separation, so often mentioned during this time of transformation, is referring to our separation from God. This has occurred as a result of the imbalance between the Masculine and Feminine Polarities of God within us. The separation of power and love created a chasm between the heart and head of Humanity. When power is not embraced with Divine Love, the imperfection of dominant, aggressive behavior begins to reflect in the person. History has clearly recorded the abuse of power and the imbalance and dominance of the masculine polarity on Earth.

Now, it is time to heal this imbalance. The Feminine Polarity of God–Divine Love–is pouring into the frequencies of Earth as never before. At this time, our God Parents are giving us every opportunity to bring these Divine energies into balance. When this occurs, we will reunite with our God Presence, and our thoughts, feelings and actions will be realigned with the Divine Plan for this blessed Planet. The HEART (LOVE)–HEAD (WISDOM)–HAND (POWER) of Humanity will function as one in alignment with the Divine Plan for the Earth.

Our opportunity during this 20 year period will be to truly balance, once and for all, the Masculine and Feminine Polarities of God within us. This will result in the re-unification of all Humanity with the Sunshine Yellow Christ Light of Enlightenment. We will become One again with our own Divinity, and we will fulfill our destiny as Sons and Daughters of God. This is the true meaning of the Second Coming of the Christ, and it is the Divine Plan for every man, woman and child on Earth.

To assure the victory of our Ascension into the Fourth Dimension, there are two necessary activities of Light. The first involves the invocation of the full power and momentum of the Seventh Ray of Spiritual Freedom, the Violet Transmuting Flame, into every electron of Humanity's misqualified energy on Earth. The second involves the affirmation and the ACCEPTANCE of our true identity, our true God reality.

Please center yourself now and join in consciousness with the entire Company of Heaven as we invoke these activities of Light.

LETTING GO INTO THE VIOLET FIRE

"I AM" now enveloped in an invincible forcefield of protection. From this focus "I AM" able to review my life as an objective observer. I ask my Higher Self to push to the surface of my conscious mind every single experience, both known and unknown, that is in any way preventing me from attaining my highest good.

Blazing in, through and around my four lower bodies (physical, etheric, mental and emotional) is the full power of the Violet Transmuting Flame. This Light from the very Heart of God instantly transmutes these negative thoughts, words, actions, feelings and memories back into their original perfection.

"I AM" at perfect Peace.

As this information surfaces, I effortlessly let it go, without emotion, without pain and without fear...into the Violet Fire.

I experience this negative energy being transmuted back into Light, and I love it FREE!

SO BE IT! BELOVED "I AM"!

THE FLAME OF LIFE

"I AM" a Being of Flame, and "I AM" Its Light.

"I AM" a part of an Activity reacquainting all human beings with their Flame and their Light.

"I AM" the Flame which is the vibration of the Godhead. "I AM" the Flame which is the cohesive love which holds the Sun and Stars in place. "I AM" the Flame whose power projects Light Rays from the Sun. "I AM" the Flame which fills all the Universe with the glory of Itself.

"I AM" the Flame, the animating principle of life. Wherever "I AM" there is God Activity. "I AM" the Alpha and Omega of Creation. "I AM" the beginning, and "I AM" the end of manifestation, all externalization. For "I AM" the Flame, which is the Source of all and into which all returns.

The Flame which "I AM" is a power. The Flame which "I AM" is a substance. The Flame which "I AM" is the all of everything: energy, vibration and consciousness in action, ever fulfilling the Divine Plan of Creation. The Flame which "I AM" shall restore this Planet Earth and set her free eternally.

The Flame which "I AM" is a Fourth Dimensional activity. The Flame which "I AM" is the Higher Law of God come to assert Its full dominion over all the lesser laws of the third dimensional world of Humanity. It is Master over every vibration less than Itself. It is all loving, all knowing and all powerful, and "I AM" that Flame in action amongst Humanity.

Within the Flame which "I AM" is every good and perfect thing; every thought and feeling the God Parents have ever had for the blessing of Their Creation. This perfection is externalized as Light. Within the Flame is the seed of all things, and within the Light is the full manifestation of all things. "I AM" the Flame, and "I AM" Its Light.

The Flame which "I AM" is available like air or water. It is everywhere present, available to those who perceive It and accept It. This is my reason for Being–the Flame and the Light embodied in a form acceptable to Humanity. "I AM" the Flame, again reaching the withering souls of Humanity, filling them with Light...the substance of myself, my Holy Self. "I AM" embodied for this reason and no other.

For "I AM" a part of an Activity designed to reacquaint all Humanity with their Flame and their Light.

"I AM" Being of Flame, and "I AM" Its Light.
"I AM" the Flame of Life.
"I AM" That "I AM".

from Group Avatar

Feel these two activities of Light being permanently sealed in through and around you, increasing daily and hourly as you repeat the affirmations.

We have all worked together at inner levels for aeons of time, and it is wonderful that we are now joining together consciously in the outer world. The gathering of Lightworkers, mentioned in this book, has occurred through two annual global conferences. We are consistently being guided by the Heavenly Realms throughout this sacred process of transformation. If you would like to have additional information and continue working with us, please write. Our address is:

The World Congress on Illumination
sponsored by

The New Age Study of Humanity's Purpose
P.O. Box 41883, Tucson, Arizona 85717   USA

and
The Group Avatar Conference
sponsored by

Group Avatar
P.O. Box 41505, Tucson, Arizona 85717   USA

EARTH'S ORBITAL ADJUSTMENT

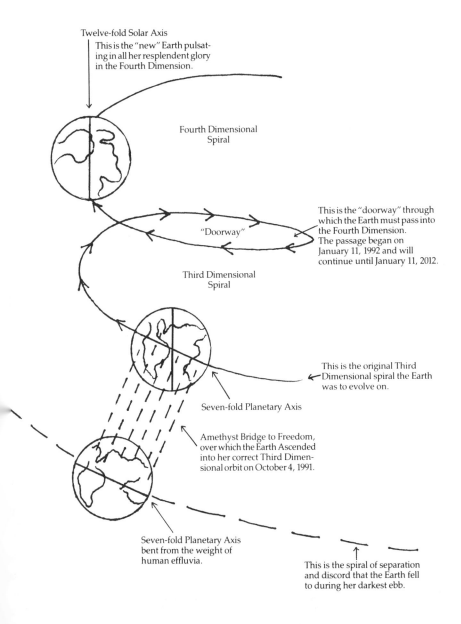

Twelve-fold Solar Axis
This is the "new" Earth pulsating in all her resplendent glory in the Fourth Dimension.

Fourth Dimensional Spiral

This is the "doorway" through which the Earth must pass into the Fourth Dimension. The passage began on January 11, 1992 and will continue until January 11, 2012.

"Doorway"

Third Dimensional Spiral

This is the original Third Dimensional spiral the Earth was to evolve on.

Seven-fold Planetary Axis

Amethyst Bridge to Freedom, over which the Earth Ascended into her correct Third Dimensional orbit on October 4, 1991.

Seven-fold Planetary Axis bent from the weight of human effluvia.

This is the spiral of separation and discord that the Earth fell to during her darkest ebb.

There is a set of three tapes associated with this chapter "You
Have Come To Save the Earth...And Your Time Is At Hand."
Part 1   Part 2   Part 3
See Page 219 for Order Form

CHAPTER
TWO

NOW IS THE OPPORTUNITY FOR
LIMITLESS PHYSICAL PERFECTION

For aeons of time, prophets, seers, religions and Holy Books have foretold of the coming of an Age when Heaven would manifest on Earth, an Age in which Humanity would develop the latent powers within and reunite with our own Divinity, an Age when transformation would occur at an atomic, cellular level, and our four lower vehicles would be changed into expressions of radiant beauty, vibrant health, eternal youth and limitless perfection.

We have contemplated this lofty vision and dreamed of such things as the rapture, resurrection, transformation and ascension. We have struggled to believe that such an awesome, supernatural phenomenon might one day occur, but I don't think we ever really thought we would be here to see it happen. As long as we held it off in the distant future, it somehow seemed like a remote possibility, but to envision such a change taking place tangibly, now in our everyday lives, seems like pure fantasy.

The truth of the matter is that transformation *is* going to occur on Earth, and when it does, it will happen with the assistance of all of the Lightworkers in embodiment at the time. Why not right here and right now? Why not with the assistance of you and me? Well, guess what? THIS IS IT!!! You and I have volunteered to be here on Earth at this Cosmic Moment because *this is the moment of our transformation into limitless physical perfection.*

This glorious event will take place, not by someone waving a wand and saying "voila," but, rather, through the normal acceleration of the physics, chemistry and biology of atomic, cellular structures in all physical matter.

As we have discussed previously, the aging, disease, disintegration and mortification we experience in our physical bodies now is a result of "the fall of man" and not part of the original Divine Plan. Originally, the plan was that we would evolve through our Earthly experience using our creative faculties of thought and feeling to learn to become masters of energy and vibration, thus becoming co-creators with our Father-Mother God, fulfilling the Universal Law of "as above, so below." When we began experimenting with our thoughts and feelings in ways that were contrary to God's Will, the discordant frequencies of vibration we were creating began to reflect first in our four lower bodies and then in the environment. This, gradually, resulted in breaking down the perfect patterns in the RNA-DNA messenger codes that form the RNA-DNA molecules which are the building blocks for all manifest form. This caused weak, distorted cellular structures to form which eventually evolved into the aging, disease, deformity, decay and death we now, unfortunately, accept as a normal part of life.

I would like to share with you, briefly, the information pouring forth from the Realms of Illumined Truth regarding our descent into physical form, what happened to our bodies during the fall and what we must do now to reclaim our path of limitless, physical perfection. The goal of Heaven is for us to understand this more clearly, so that the opportunity being presented to us now will register in our minds as viable and practical rather than supernatural and unattainable.

OUR DESCENT INTO MATTER
Solar Vehicles

At the moment of our inception, we were breathed forth from the Immortal Three-fold Flame of our Father-Mother God into unformed primal Light substance. There, our God Parents commanded the Universal Light to clothe us in our own Immortal Victorious Three-fold Flame. Around our Flame, They projected a radiant forcefield of Light, a blazing Sun which formed the initial impulse of our Solar vehicles. This was our resplendent White Fire Being. (See illustration page 139.) Within the blazing Sun of our White Fire Being, we began to form the duality of Divinity, a Feminine Polarity of

Divine Love and a Masculine Polarity of Divine Power. These two Polarities of God began to pulsate within our Solar vehicles as an individualized Presence known as "I AM". (See illustration page 141.)

Once we stood forth individualized as "I AM", we were ready to experience the perfection of the Causal Body of God. The Causal Body of God, as far as our present experience is concerned, contains twelve spheres of Divinity known as the twelve Solar Aspects of Deity. These Solar Aspects contain the Divine Qualities of God, as well as Sacred Knowledge, Music, Colors, Fragrances and Cosmic Tones to enhance the involutionary and evolutionary experience of all evolving life forms.

To begin the descent into the individualized experience of a Son or Daughter of God, our "I AM" Presence stepped forth into the first sphere of God's Causal Body, the Sapphire Blue First Aspect of Deity. Within this sphere, our "I AM" Presence absorbed the wisdom and knowledge contained within that Aspect of God, and a band of Blue Light formed around the "I AM" Presence, creating the first band of our own Causal Body. The Light was then anchored along the Solar Spine of our "I AM" Presence, creating the first Solar Chakra. Through this Solar Chakra, the God Qualities of the First Aspect of Deity: God's Will, Illumined Faith, Power, Protection and Victory began flowing into the spheres of influence of our "I AM" Presence.

This process continued through the remaining eleven spheres of the Causal Body of God, and upon completion, our God Presence had formed a Twelve-fold Causal Body of Its own, which was radiating in oneness with the Causal Body of God. A Twelve-fold Solar Spine reflecting the Twelve-fold Aspect of Deity was also formed to transmit the perfection of God into the evolving experience of our "I AM" Presence.

The Twelve-fold Causal Body and Solar Spine reflect the following Aspects of Divinity.

FIRST ASPECT–BLUE–GOD'S WILL, ILLUMINED FAITH, POWER, PROTECTION, VICTORY

SECOND ASPECT–YELLOW–ENLIGHTENMENT, ILLU-
MINATION, UNDERSTANDING, WISDOM

THIRD ASPECT–PINK–DIVINE LOVE

FOURTH ASPECT–WHITE–PURITY, HOPE, THE IMMAC-
ULATE CONCEPT, RESURRECTION, ASCENSION

FIFTH ASPECT–GREEN–TRUTH,   CONSECRATION,
DEDICATION, CONCENTRATION, HEALING, IN-
NER VISION

SIXTH ASPECT–RUBY–MINISTERING GRACE, DEVO-
TIONAL WORSHIP, PEACE, HEALING

SEVENTH ASPECT–VIOLET–FREEDOM, FORGIVENESS,
MERCY, COMPASSION, JUSTICE, OPPORTUNITY,
TRANSMUTATION, LIBERTY

EIGHTH ASPECT–AQUAMARINE–CLARITY

NINTH ASPECT–MAGENTA–HARMONY, BALANCE

TENTH ASPECT–GOLD–ETERNAL PEACE, ABUNDANCE,
OPULENCE, FINANCIAL FREEDOM, PROSPERITY

ELEVENTH ASPECT–PEACH–DIVINE PURPOSE, JOY,
ENTHUSIASM

TWELFTH ASPECT–OPAL–TRANSFORMATION
(See illustration page 143.)

After the formation of our Solar garments of Light:

we were ready for the next step which was our descent into
physical matter.

Planetary Vehicles

In order to experience the third dimensional, physical plane, our God Presence needed to create a stepped down transformer that could navigate in the denseness of physical matter while our "I AM" Presence remained in the more rarified frequencies of the Fourth Dimension. Thus, the Holy Christ Self was created.

Our "I AM" Presence projected into the stepped down frequencies of the third dimensional plane a replica of Itself, which was enveloped in an Immortal Victorious Three-fold Flame. This aspect of our own being is known as the Holy Christ Self, and It is "the mediator between God and man" (see illustration page 145). Our "I Am" Presence sustained the Holy Christ Self and the Three-fold Flame in the third dimension by projecting Light into Them from Its Twelve-fold Solar Spine.

The Twelve-fold Solar Spine was reflected into the spinal column of the Holy Christ Self in a unique activity of Divine Alchemy. Our "I AM" Presence blends the aspects of the Solar Spine into a unified forcefield of Light known as the Circle of the Sacred Twelve. It is then projected into third dimensional frequencies, and, as it passes through the spiral prism from the Fourth Dimension into the third dimension, it is stepped down in frequency and divided into the seven-fold physical spectrum of Light that we see in the rainbow. This Light then manifests along the axis of our physical vehicles as a seven-fold planetary spine with seven major chakras. It also forms a seven-fold Causal Body that surrounds the Holy Christ Self. Beginning with the crown chakra and continuing to the root chakra at the base of the spine, the seven-fold planetary spine reflects the physical colors of violet, indigo, blue, green, yellow, orange and red (see illustration page 147).

Once the planetary spine and seven-fold Causal Body were formed, our Holy Christ Self began to draw elemental substance around Itself. This formed the physical vehicles It would use to traverse the Earth in Its quest to become master of physical matter through the use of the creative faculties of thought and feeling. These vehicles are known as the four lower bodies–physical, etheric, mental and emotional (see illustration page 149).

In order to energize and sustain the elemental substance the four lower bodies are made of, our Holy Christ Self magnetized from our "I AM" Presence the Divine Light that would form a generating vortex of energy within each body.

The first elemental vortex was formed about twelve inches above the head of the Holy Christ Self. This was the Spirit or ether vortex, which was created to energize pure spiritual energies from our "I AM" Presence into the elemental substance of our four lower bodies (see illustration page 112). Next, the air vortex was formed in the area of the throat of the Holy Christ Self. This vortex drew pure spiritual Light to energize our *etheric body* (see illustration page 115). The fire vortex was created in the area of the mid-chest of the Holy Christ Self, and it energized our *mental body* (see illustration page 118). The water vortex was formed at the base of the spine of our Holy Christ Self, and it energized the *emotional body* (see illustration page 121). Finally, the earth vortex was created at the point between the feet of our Holy Christ Self, and it energized our *physical body* (see illustration page 127).

The formation of the elemental vortexes completed our vehicles of Earthly experience:

1. Our Holy Christ Self enveloped in the Immortal, Victorious Three-fold Flame. Page 145

2. Our seven-fold Causal Body and our planetary spine, which reflects the Solar Light of the Circle of the Sacred Twelve into the seven-fold physical spectrum of Light and color. Page 147

3. Our four lower bodies–physical, etheric, mental and emotional–which our Holy Christ Self and Three-fold Flame use to experience the physical plane of Earth. Page 149

4. The five elemental vortexes that energize and rejuvenate our four lower bodies. Page 151

Originally, our Holy Christ Self and our Three-fold Flame were as large as our four lower bodies, and They engulfed our physical, etheric, mental and emotional vehicles with Their radiance and Light. The Holy Christ Self was the master of these vehicles and directed them to obey. Our mental body thought only the thoughts projected through it from the Holy Christ Self. Our emotional body felt only the feelings of Divine Love and Harmony that were expressed through the Holy Christ Self. Our physical body navigated around in the physical plane and acted only under the command of the Holy Christ Self, and our etheric body continually recorded our Earthly experiences as it reflected the perfect patterns of the Holy Christ Self into the cells and organs of the physical body enabling them to outpicture perfection.

The elemental vortexes continually replenished the pure Light in the elements of the four lower bodies allowing them to always maintain eternal youth, vibrant health and radiant beauty.

This is how Humanity evolved on Earth prior to the "fall," and this is what we must return to now in order to progress into our next step of evolution with the rest of our Solar System.

As we begin to truly grasp this information, we will understand with greater clarity how complex we actually are. We are *multi-dimensional* beings, functioning on many levels and through various vehicles simultaneously. We are not just this limited physical body that we have erroneously identified with. That notion developed as a result of the fall and our separation from our own Divinity.

THE FALL AND SEPARATION FROM OUR OWN DIVINITY

In the original Divine Plan, the purpose for coming into the third dimensional plane of Earth was to give our Holy Christ Self the opportunity to use the creative faculties of thought and feeling to become master of physical energy.

Through the process of thought and feeling, our Holy Christ Self would take unformed primal Light substance and bring it into manifest form as it reflected on the atomic and sub-atomic particles of physical matter. What we held in our consciousness, we brought into form. The Holy Christ Self, at that time, was in constant communion with the "I AM" Presence, and, therefore, the thoughts and feelings It directed through the four lower bodies were always reflecting the perfection of the Heavenly Fourth Dimensional Realms. This enabled the Universal Law of "as above, so below" to become a physical reality. At that point in our evolutionary journey, we were fulfilling our potential as Sons and Daughters of God. We were created in God's Image, destined to become co-creators with God, and we used our gift of free will to expand the borders of our Father's Kingdom in the world of form.

For a while, we fulfilled that destiny in perfect Divine Order, but, unfortunately, at a particular point in time, Humanity became curious about the commandment of our God Parents. Why should we not partake of the tree of knowledge of good and evil? What will happen? What is evil? Eventually, our curiosity became too much to withstand, and we began experimenting with our thoughts and feelings in ways that were not in alignment with God's Will. The intelligence within our mental body began forming thoughts separately from the directives of the Holy Christ Self. Our emotional body began translating those thoughts into feelings that were not expressed by the Holy Christ Self, and the physical body began acting out the thoughts and feelings without the consent of the Holy Christ Self. The etheric body recorded the distorted patterns of the thoughts and feelings, and the discord began to reflect on the cells and organs of the physical body. This process continued until the four lower bodies actually developed a separate personality that controlled them and operated *in opposition* to the directives of the Holy Christ Self. We refer to this personality now as the *human ego*.

When the human ego arrogantly took command of our four lower bodies, our Holy Christ Self had no choice but to stand by and watch. Not even the highest aspect of our own Divinity has the authority to interfere with our gift of free will. Gradually, as a merciful activity of life, our Holy Christ Self began withdrawing the Light It was projecting through our four lower bodies from our "I AM" Presence, so that we would have less energy to distort with our negative thoughts and feelings. This caused our Three-fold Flame to become smaller and smaller until it eventually shrunk to a mere fraction of an inch in our heart. The tremendous shaft of Light that used to pour through our seven-fold planetary spine from the Twelve-fold Solar Spine of our God Presence became the thin stream of Light we now refer to as the silver cord (see illustration page 149). This act of mercy saved us from our own self-destruction, but it tragically cut us off to a great degree from our Source.

Our four lower bodies became denser and denser as our negative energy began interpenetrating our cellular structures at an atomic level. This distortion began reflecting as decay, disintegration, disease and death. We fell into denser and denser octaves of matter until the elemental vortexes could no longer rejuvenate the elements of the four lower bodies. This caused the phenomenon we experience now as aging. Instead of the elemental vortexes recharging our cells throughout our lifetime as originally intended, we come to Earth with charged cells that regenerate effectively for approximately 25 years. Then, just like a battery that is not recharged, the process becomes weaker and weaker until the cells gradually become less vibrant and healthy as time goes on. They finally die altogether in about 70 or 80 years.

This sad state of affairs actually buried us in such a sea of negativity that we were separated in consciousness from our Holy Christ Self; we lost our way, and we forgot about our purpose and reason for being. We forgot about our own Divinity, and we forgot we were Sons and Daughters of God. This deplorable event caused us to look at the physical plane as the only reality. We thought our limited physical body and human ego were all we really were. We began to believe that the pain and suffering existing on Earth were part of God's plan instead of just being the result of misusing our thoughts and feelings. We have been struggling in the muck and mire so long that we don't believe we have a choice anymore. Most of Humanity feels victimized and pitiful. They feel hopeless and desperate. They feel life on Earth is doomed, and there is no turning back from our path of self-destruction. *Well, enough is enough.* We have bought this lie and lived in this confusion long enough. We have played the absurd game of poverty, disease, hate, war, crime, aging, death and all other forms of limitation as long as we need to. Actually, we've played the game millions of years longer than we needed to. In Ages past, we struggled to get our heads above the mud puddle long enough to see the Light at the end of the tunnel, but we had relatively little success. The Light at the end of the tunnel was often an oncoming train.

THIS TIME IT IS GOING TO BE DIFFERENT!! THIS TIME WE ARE GOING TO SUCCEED *VICTORIOUSLY!*

Doesn't that sound wonderful? I know many of you are saying "yes," but you really don't believe it will happen. We are often afraid to dare to accept such glorious ideas for fear of being disappointed. Fortunately, we don't have to completely accept it at this time. We don't have to believe it. We don't even have to understand it. All we need to do is experiment with the tools that have been revealed to us through the gift of Sacred Knowledge from the Realms of Illumined Truth, and we will prove it to ourselves beyond a shadow of a doubt.

RETURNING TO CHRIST CONSCIOUSNESS

The Divine Birthright for this Planet is the manifestation of Heaven on Earth, and the first step in accomplishing that goal is healing the self-inflicted separation from our Holy Christ Self. This will be an individual and a collective accomplishment for all Humanity. Even though we are receiving more assistance from on High than ever before in the history of time, this healing will not be the result of Divine Intervention. It will occur only through the personal, conscious, cooperative efforts of those abiding in the physical plane. Humanity created the separation from the Holy Christ Self through the abuse of free will, and Karmic Law dictates that Humanity alone can heal that separation. It is true that we, in the physical plane, are being given every conceivable tool to enhance our ability to succeed, but the ultimate responsibility is ours.

We must transform the human ego and transmute the dense negativity that is interpenetrating the cells, atoms and molecules of the four lower bodies. We must raise the vibration of the four lower bodies up out of the frequencies of decay and disintegration into the embrace and control of our Holy Christ Self once again. Regardless of who we are or where we have come from, the Lightworkers have volunteered to accomplish this mighty feat as an example for others to follow. Through this process, we will blaze an omnipotent pathway of Light into Cosmic Christ Consciousness. We have deliberately become part of the fallen energies on Earth with the explicit goal of lifting these energies up as we return to Christ Consciousness. The Cosmic Moment for us to fulfill that mission is NOW.

With the quantum leaps in vibration we have taken since Harmonic Convergence, and with the transmutation of 50% of the negativity on Earth that was accomplished during the Solar Eclipse on July 11, 1991, we are now ready to ascend into Christ Consciousness. On January 11, 1992, we began our ascent through the doorway into the Fourth Dimension. The Earth is ascending into a new Spiral of Solar Identity. This process will take approximately 20 years in our Earthly time-space compendium until the year 2012. During that time, we are being given the unparalleled opportunity to transform our four lower bodies into their original Divine intent. For the first time since prior to the fall of man, we are actually in a position where this transformation can occur easily at an atomic cellular level. The Spiritual Axis of the Earth has now been straightened, and we are once again in alignment to receive Divine Solar Energies. Our physical spinal columns have also been brought into alignment to receive spiritual energies from our Holy Christ Self. Prior to this occurrence, it was practically impossible for us to lift up in vibration into the Light Body of our Holy Christ Self, but now it is very possible, not only possible, but a necessary, critical part of our Divine Plan.

I know it is difficult for us to fully understand the magnitude of what all of this really means, but, fortunately, our intellectual comprehension is not necessary for us to succeed in returning to Christ Consciousness. All we have to do is be *willing* to ascend into our glorious Holy Christ Self and relinquish the control our human ego has over our four lower bodies. We have been given wonderful exercises, initiations, visualizations and tools that will accelerate the process. If we will just experiment with them daily, we will begin to see results immediately. These gifts are scientific and utilize the frequencies and vibrations of the Realms of God's First Cause of Perfection. The Divine Fiat has been issued that *limitless physical perfection* must now manifest on Earth. This means through every particle of life. As you and I begin applying the Divine Gifts that have been given to us to accomplish this transformation, our friends and loved ones will become aware of the truth of their effectiveness. Then, they will be trusting enough to apply them to their own lives. The effect will be exponential until every man, woman and child returns to the perfection of their Holy Christ Self. At that point, the perfect thoughts and feelings of our collective Holy Christ Selves will reflect on the physical plane of Earth, and the environment and all of the kingdoms of nature will likewise begin outpicturing the Perfection of God's First Cause. Then, Heaven will truly be manifest on Earth, and we will have victoriously reclaimed our direction.

THE SECOND COMING OF THE CHRIST

As a result of the human ego seizing and taking control of our four lower bodies, these vehicles are filled with dense, destructive frequencies of negative thoughts, words, feelings and actions. If we could see this negative energy with our physical sight, it would look like black, gummy tar oozing in, through and around the cells, molecules, atoms and electrons of our physical, etheric, mental and emotional bodies. This distorted energy sticks to the electrons and weighs them down, thus preventing them from vibrating at a frequency of harmony and vibrant health. The tar-like negativity cloaks the electrons and blocks their natural transmission of Light. Consequently, the electrons vibrate slower and become heavier, darker and denser. This process is what actually separated the four lower bodies from the Holy Christ Self. As the four lower bodies became contaminated with heavy negative energy, they dropped away from the Holy Christ Self and fell into a frequency of discord far below the Octave of the Holy Christ Self.

Even though the Holy Christ Self continually tried to stay in contact with our four lower vehicles and tried to guide them back into Its embrace and direction, the clamor and rampage of the human ego prevented us from hearing the "still, small voice within." We heard only the distorted commands of the human ego which always acts on a whim to gratify the appetites of the physical senses. This created a self-perpetuating process that catapulted us deeper into the chasm of darkness and despair. It propelled us on a downward spiral into oblivion that we must now finally stop.

At the inception of the last Age 2000 years ago, it was obvious that Humanity had truly lost our way. It was determined by God that a dramatic event needed to occur to get our attention and reveal to us the pathway Home to our Holy Christ Self. A radiant Being of Light volunteered to come to Earth and reveal to Humanity the Love of God and the way to return to the Christ. Most of Beloved Jesus' mission was misunderstood, and He knew that it would be. That is why He said not then, but at the time of His Second Coming, the Earth would be transformed.

Many of the world religions are still misunderstanding Jesus' words, and they are, consequently, vehemently resisting the Sacred Knowledge appearing on the screen of life. For instance, Jesus was referring to the wayward human ego and the resulting destructive behavior patterns of the four lower bodies when He said mankind had become "evil." This has been misinterpreted by some religions as *Humanity* being innately evil. Because of this inaccurate interpretation, they believe it is blasphemous for us to proclaim God is within our hearts or for us to believe we are Sons and Daughters of God. Ironically, unless we accept our own Divinity and acknowledge that we are Sons and Daughters of God, we will not fulfill our Divine Plan or be able to return to our Father-Mother God as individualized expressions of radiant Light, which was the reason for our creation in the first place.

Jesus also taught that unless the human ego surrenders and allows the Holy Christ Self to take full dominion of the four lower bodies again, there is no way we can return to our Father-Mother God. Jesus showed, through His example, the path of Divine Love which will be the natural consequence when the Holy Christ Self is in command of our lower vehicles.

Again, this message was very misunderstood, and some of the world religions believe that Jesus did it for us, when in fact, He came to show us the path of Divine Love that we must follow in order to lift our bodies up and heal the separation from our Holy Christ Self. Some believe that all we have to do is accept Jesus as our personal savior, and everything will be done for us. But, this belief system is in conflict with all of the Divine Laws of the Universe. *No one can do it for us.* Our gift of life is a Sacred Trust, and we are responsible for how we use every electron of precious life energy. If we have contaminated its perfect vibration through the misuse of our thoughts, words, actions or feelings, we alone are obligated to transmute the discord back into Light. Even the all-encompassing Presence of God will only show us the way and then allow us to use our free will to choose our level of compliance.

Interestingly, the religions that are teaching that the Sacred Knowledge of the New Age of Enlightenment is the "work of the devil" or that one must accept Jesus as his/her personal savior or "burn in hell forever," are the very religions that are being misguided by the treachery of the human ego and the forces of imbalance. If anything is the so-called "work of the devil," it is perpetuating the belief that someone else has accepted responsibility for our misdeeds, and we can just go on being led astray by our human ego with no responsibility to life for our actions. The forces of imbalance operate in the discord of deception, and the misinformation and disinformation being buffeted about in the world religions at this time are obviously part of the futile attempt to stop the forward progress of Humanity's ascent back into Christhood.

The hypocrisy surfacing in the religions is part of the purging of these "end times." Beloved Jesus warned us, "You will hear, lo, I am here, and lo, I am there, BUT BY THEIR WORKS ALONE SHALL THEY BE KNOWN."

So...contrary to popular belief, the Second Coming is not going to be Jesus riding into the atmosphere of Earth on a white cloud, wielding His power to supercede our free will and fix everything for us as He gathers up in one arm those who have uttered the words "I accept Jesus as my personal savior," while He casts everyone else (regardless of how Christlike their lives may have been) into the burning inferno of hell for eternity. Knowing the Divine Order of the Universe and the depth of God's compassion, mercy and love, it is truly mind boggling that we could have ever been duped by the human ego and the forces of imbalance into believing such a ludicrous thing.

In reality, the Second Coming is simple and obvious in the Light of Truth pouring forth from the Divine Mind of God. The Second Coming of the Christ will occur individually for each person on the Planet when we command the human ego into the Light, and it surrenders its influence over our four lower bodies. Then, once again, our physical, etheric, mental and emotional vehicles will be transmuted by Sacred Fire, and they will ascend in frequency and vibration back into the Light Body of our Holy Christ Self. This will enable the elemental vortexes to once again replenish and rejuvenate our vehicles, restoring them to vibrant health, radiant beauty and eternal youth as originally intended. Our Holy Christ Self will take full dominion of all of the aspects of our Earthly existence, and our Immortal Victorious Three-fold Flame will once again expand to envelop our vehicles as the Circle of the Sacred Twelve from the Solar Spine of our "I AM" Presence begins to reflect effectively, once more, through our seven-fold planetary spine of physical expression. At that moment of Divine Alchemy, our self-inflicted separation from God and our own Divinity will be eternally healed, and we will be "born again" into the Christ Consciousness of the new Heaven and the new Earth.

This Ascension activity of Divine Alchemy is available to us *here* and *now*. It is going to be an individual and a collective Ascension into the Light. The 20-year period we are now in is providing a window of opportunity that will make it easier than ever (since prior to the fall of man) to regain our direction and reclaim our Divinity. We have been given the Sacred Knowledge to accomplish our mission, and by utilizing the tools and agreeing to be the pioneers, we will blaze a Mighty Highway of Light into Christhood for all Humanity to follow. Then, the victory of the Second Coming of the Christ will be a manifest fact, and this sweet Earth and all her life will Ascend into the next spiral of perfection to continue our evolutionary journey back to the Heart of God.

THE PHYSICAL TRANSFORMATION OF OUR FOUR LOWER BODIES

Once the Holy Christ Self and our Three-fold Flame have again taken full dominion of our four lower vehicles, our tangible, physical transformation will naturally occur. Remember, we are returning this sweet Earth to her original Divine Plan, and in the beginning, this Planet was created in the perfection of the Garden of Eden. This Planet began as an opportunity to see how the Fourth Dimensional Realms of Glory and Perfection might manifest in the density of form. This was an experiment to prove the Universal Law of "as above, so below." There are many realms and dimensions that express the perfection of Divinity throughout the whole of creation, but through all eternity, the third dimensional physical realm is unique. It provides an opportunity for physical mastery over energy and matter that is not available in any other dimension.

The uniqueness of the physical realm is that in this frequency the free flowing, unformed Universal primal Light that fills all realms and dimensions allows itself to be fixed in particular structures and patterns until the evolving individualized aspect of God, the Holy Christ Self, completes the learning opportunity of that particular manifest experience. The fixed patterns are called atoms, and they are the basis of all physical form. Atoms are fixed into molecules, and molecules are fixed into cells and organs, which are fixed into our four lower bodies. The atom remains central to all physical form.

Within the core of every atom is the Sacred Solar Fire of Creation which contains within It the *LIMITLESS POTENTIAL OF PERFECTION* that is expressed in every other Divine Realm. This Sacred Fire was originally under the natural dominion and influence of the Holy Christ Self and the Immortal Victorious Three-fold Flame of Divine Love, Wisdom and Power. When the human ego took command of the four lower bodies, the Solar Force of Creation within the core of the atom was unleashed in ways that actually destroyed manifest form rather than perpetuating it. Our nuclear and atomic weapons of mass destruction are extreme graphic examples of the miscreation of the human ego. The original intent of creation was that the Sacred Solar Fire of Creation within the atoms would be influenced solely by the Holy Christ Self and the Three-fold Flame. When that is the case, atomic energy is released only in cooperation and loving unity with all other manifest form. Then, this limitless source of energy within the atom is harnessed to refine and perfect the physical universe instead of destroying it.

The original Divine Blueprint that reflects the Sacred Knowledge that limitless perfection is not only possible but necessary in order to complete our Earthly experiment is still reverberating as a profound memory within the RNA-DNA patterns of our cellular structures. When our Holy Christ Self and our Three-fold Flame begin to take control of our four lower bodies and, once again, express Themselves from within the Sacred Solar Fire of Creation in the core of every atom, the RNA-DNA patterns of perfection will be activated. Then, the atoms of our four lower bodies will be transformed, and limitless physical perfection will be tangibly experienced in our everyday lives.

THE ELEMENTAL SUBSTANCE
OF OUR FOUR LOWER BODIES

The Solar Eclipse of July 11, 1991, and the resulting Solar Inbreath raised the vibration of all elemental substance on Earth. This created an environment that enabled the intelligence within all elemental forms: ether, air, fire, water and earth, to reach up and receive greater frequencies of Solar Light. Now, there is a tremendous opportunity for the healing and restoration of our physical vehicles. The Divine Beings, known as the Directors of the Elements, are inspiring the commitment within all intelligent elemental life to refine the physical patterns which they currently manifest. This includes our four lower bodies. If we will simply allow our Three-fold Flames and our Holy Christ Selves to have full dominion of our physical/earth, etheric/air, mental/fire and emotional/water bodies, the intelligent elemental substance that comprises our actual cells will cooperate with us, and our four lower bodies will be transformed into the perfection of our Holy Christ Self.

The intelligent elemental life forms in each of the five elements are referred to as Elementals. These beings use atoms as their building blocks. Every atom is like a miniature Universe, and, just as a Universe or Planet has a Divine Being that oversees its evolution, so does each atom. There is an Elemental Being that maintains the forcefield of each atom, molecule, cell and organ. For our entire physical body, there is a Master Deva, known as the *Body Elemental*. These intelligent beings have been struggling to hold on to the Divine Blueprint for our four lower bodies since we first fell into the chaos of the human ego aeons ago. They have been patiently awaiting our decision to reclaim the authority the human ego usurped and return full dominion of our four lower bodies to our Holy Christ Self and our Three-fold Flame.

Each Elemental being has been indelibly stamped with the patterns of physical perfection. This is true, even though the physical substance of Earth has fallen out of balance. The key that will enable the Elementals to, once again, outpicture the perfection they know is the expansion of our Holy Christ Self and our Three-fold Flame. The more we function within the radiance of these two Divine Light Bodies, the more the Elemental Beings within our four lower vehicles are empowered to re-align the atomic/cellular substance that makes up those vehicles. The Three-fold Flame is used by the Elementals as an atomic accelerator, and, through this forcefield of Divinity, the physical substance of our Earthly bodies is swept up in energy, vibration and consciousness as it is transformed into *Electronic Light Substance*. In this frequency of Light, our bodies will outpicture perfect health, eternal youth, radiant beauty, opulence, abundance and every other aspect of God's Perfection.

This is not a vision for some distant time. This is available for each and every one of us NOW! This is the window of opportunity being presented to us by our Father-Mother God. Imagine, Humanity's Spiritual FREEDOM and limitless physical perfection now made manifest through the loving cooperation of Humanity, Elementals and Angels.

TOOLS FOR THE SECOND COMING OF THE CHRIST AND LIMITLESS PHYSICAL PERFECTION

The Violet Transmuting Flame

Within the Causal Body of God pulsates the Seventh Aspect of Deity, which vibrates with the Divine Qualities of Forgiveness, Mercy, Compassion, Transmutation, Freedom, Justice and Opportunity. This sacred Violet Light will be the predominant influence on the Planet for the dawning New Age of Aquarius, which will last approximately 2000 years. The Divine Violet Fire is projected from the Causal Body of God into the forcefield of Aquarius where it is energized and amplified prior to flowing into the atmosphere of Earth. It is largely because of this precious gift of Light that our transformation in this Cosmic Moment has been assured. The specific frequency of transmutation contained within this Sacred Violet Fire is a merciful gift of Light that works as an atomic accelerator. Upon our invocation, it actually penetrates into the black, gummy tar-like substance of our misqualified negative energy and transmutes it back into Light. This is a tool more powerful than our finite minds can conceive. Under the direction of our Holy Christ Self and our "I AM" Presence, the Violet Transmuting Flame will actually transmute every electron of precious life energy we have ever misqualified in any time frame or existence, both known and unknown. This literally means that the heavy negative energy that is interpenetrating the atoms, molecules, cells and organs of our four lower bodies, keeping them in a state of aging and decay, can now be completely removed and transmuted back into Light. When this occurs, our four lower bodies will be able to easily ascend back into the embrace of our Holy Christ Self, and they will return to their Divine purpose and intent. Instead of being used to gratify the excessive appetites of the human ego, they will be used to express the perfection of our own Divinity. Then, we will truly experience what *limitless physical perfection* really means. This concept is often contemplated but rarely ever accepted as a possibility. Now, we are being asked as Lightworkers to prove it to Humanity, and, through our concentrated efforts, so we shall.

The following invocations and visualizations are simple, but incredibly powerful and effective. If we will use them DAILY AND RHYTHMICALLY (approximately the same time each day), the Violet Transmuting Flame will build in momentum in our everyday lives and experiences, and we will soon see tangible proof of our own transformation. Our friends and loved ones will begin to witness the improvement in our quality of life and the restoration of our physical bodies. Then, through our example, we can effectively share with them the truth of the Sacred Knowledge of the Violet Transmuting Flame and the other Divine Gifts of Transformation.

The Power of Invocation

Even though the Violet Transmuting Flame is filling the atmosphere of Earth, in order for us to experience it personally in our own lives, we must draw it into our Heart Flame through the power of invocation. The Universal Law is THE CALL FOR ASSISTANCE MUST COME FROM THE REALM WHERE THE ASSISTANCE IS NEEDED. If we will invoke the Violet Flame through the power of our own Divinity, our "I AM" Presence and our Holy Christ Self, it will obey our command and fulfill our decree. It is a Cosmic Law that the Divine Light of God must obey the command of the Divinity in our hearts. "ASK AND YOU SHALL RECEIVE."

If we will invoke the Violet Transmuting Flame rhythmically and continually, it will blaze in, through and around the atomic cellular structures of our four lower bodies and transmute the negativity that is now cloaking the electrons. The aging, disease, disintegration and decay of our four lower bodies only exists because the accumulated negativity of our past thoughts, words, actions and feelings is contaminating the molecular structures so intensely that it is preventing the Divine patterns contained within the RNA-DNA codes from being expressed.

Any negative pattern manifesting in any one of our four lower bodies, physical, etheric, mental or emotional, is only being sustained because we are either consciously or subconsciously allowing destructive thoughts or feelings to pass through that vehicle more rhythmically and with more power than we do the Violet Transmuting Flame.

In order to eliminate the degeneration of our four lower bodies, we must rhythmically demand and command our "I AM" Presence and our Holy Christ Self to blaze and blaze and blaze the Violet Fire of Transmutation in, through and around every electron of those vehicles constantly. The Violet Fire *must* become a greater force in our consciousness than *ANY* physical limitation or outer situation, no matter how distressing or repetitive the challenge may be. Through this discipline and self-mastery, we will return our four lower vehicles to the full dominion and control of our Holy Christ Self, so they will once again follow the Divine directive they originally volunteered to serve.

The forcefield of Violet Fire surrounding our physical vehicles will eventually be so powerful that it will disallow the manifestation of any form of imbalance or degeneration. Then, *limitless physical perfection* will be a manifest reality in our lives, both tangibly and permanently.

Decrees and Visualizations

I invoke my mighty "I AM" Presence and my Holy Christ Self to empower and intensify these decrees and visualizations with the Light of a thousand Suns, increasing them daily and hourly the maximum that Cosmic Law will allow.

1. "I AM" A FORCE OF VIOLET FIRE MORE POWER-
   FUL THAN ANY HUMAN CREATION. (repeat 3
   times)

2. Through the Power of God pulsating in every human
   heart...

   I invoke the full gathered momentum of the Violet
   Transmuting Flame of Forgiveness.

   Sacred Flame, come forth NOW from the very Heart
   of God and blaze in, through and around every electron of precious life energy Humanity has ever released which is less than God's Perfection.
   Transmute NOW cause, core, effect, record and memory every thought, word, action or feeling we have
   ever expressed which prevents us from KNOWING
   and ACCEPTING our true God reality. I ask that this
   Violet Flame of Forgiveness continue to blaze through
   all life, expanding moment to moment the maximum
   that Cosmic Law will allow, until all Humanity is Free
   from every pattern or belief less than the reality of
   their God Presence.

   "I AM" the Presence of God made manifest in the
   physical world of form, and I ACCEPT my Divine reality NOW! SO BE IT! "I AM"!

3. IN THE NAME AND THE AUTHORITY OF THE
   POWER AND PRESENCE OF GOD "I AM"... BE-
   LOVED LEGIONS OF LIGHT CONCERNED WITH
   THE VIOLET FIRE AND THE SEVENTH RAY TO
   OUR EARTH...

   *EXPAND! EXPAND! AND INTENSIFY DAILY THE
   MIGHTIEST ACTION OF VIOLET FIRE in, through
   and around every electron that make up the atoms of
   our emotional, mental, etheric and physical vehicles,
   until they outpicture the God Perfection of the Holy
   Christ Self.

                              (repeat 3 times from *)
   Hold it sustained and double it each hour.
   In God's Most Holy Name "I AM".

4. LEGIONS OF THE VIOLET FIRE...BLAZE, BLAZE, BLAZE THE VIOLET FIRE OF FREEDOM'S LOVE AND TRANSMUTATION AS OF A THOUSAND SUNS IN, THROUGH AND AROUND...All Humanity, so that each Lifestream may individually acknowledge and accept the IMMACULATE CONCEPT of his/her own Holy Christ Self.

Blaze the Violet Light of a thousand Suns through every part of my physical, etheric, mental and emotional bodies and those of all Humanity. Hold it sustained until all human creation there, its cause and core, is dissolved and transmuted into purity and perfection.

5. THE VICTORIOUS VIOLET FIRE OF FREEDOM'S LOVE now...Heals our bodies...

Harmonizes and stabilizes our feelings...illumines our consciousness and sets us FREE...raising us into full mastery over all human appearances, desires, feelings and limitations, now and forever sustained.

(repeat 3 times)

6. THE DECREE TO THE PRECIOUS ELECTRONS
In the Name of the Almighty Presence of God "I AM", and through the full power of the Three-fold Flame pulsating in my heart, I speak directly to the intelligence within every electron of precious life energy now existing in my world. Blessed Ones, through the Power of God, I command that the Sacred Solar Fire of Creation blazing in the central core of your Being EXPAND, EXPAND, and EXPAND continuously and permanently.

I direct the Violet Transmuting Flame NOW to remove the effluvia (shadows) cloaking the electrons of my four lower bodies and every single electron existing in my environment.

Oh, Sacred Violet Flame, transmute into Light every rate of vibration which is discordant and all vibrations causing any form of limitation in my life.

In God's Most Holy Name "I AM", I command that this be accomplished NOW, even as I call, through the most powerful action of the Violet Flame ever known on Earth. I decree and experience this very moment the Violet Transmuting Flame blazing in every electron until that which is limitation can no longer exist. As the vibratory rate of each electron is quickened, the cloak of darkness is cast aside, and the shadows created by my past misuse of God's Precious Gift of Life are instantly transmuted into radiant Light.

I accept this done NOW with full power, to be daily increased with my every call...So Be It!..."I AM".

7. *Cleansing Exercise*
Stand in your room and call the Violet Transmuting Flame into action in, through and around you for at least nine feet in every direction. Raise your hands and ask your Higher Self, your God Presence, to qualify your hands with the purifying power of the Violet Transmuting Flame. Visualize your hands blazing with Violet Light–pulsating as Amethyst Suns.

Then, starting at your head, pass your hands down over your body to the feet, taking in as much of the body surface as you can reach with your hands. Envision that your hands are mighty magnets, pulling every electron of negativity out of your body.

Now, with the left hand, sweep down over the right shoulder, arm and hand, and with the right hand, give the left shoulder, arm and hand the same treatment.

Repeat this activity in its entirety four times, once for each of the four lower vehicles (physical, etheric, mental and emotional). Periodically shake your hands from the wrist to cast off the heavy, discordant energy that is being removed from your bodies and visualize the negative energy being transmuted in the surrounding Violet Fire.

If not just yet, eventually, you will be able to see with the inner sight what takes place during this exercise. In the first part of the exercise, it is as though a close fitting garment of dark substance is being removed from the body with the hands. The second time you go over the body, the "garment" removed is of a grey substance. The third time, it is of a lighter grey color, and the fourth time, even lighter. Day after day, as you proceed with the exercise, this astral substance becomes lighter and lighter in color and texture until it is entirely removed from the body.

This is real substance–with actual color, vibration and feeling, created through the misuse of energy throughout our Earthly sojourn.

On completion of the exercise, visualize the Violet Transmuting Flame expanding through your Heart Flame, flooding the entire Planet and affirm:

Beloved Holy Christ Self... EXPAND! EXPAND! AND INTENSIFY DAILY THE MIGHTIEST ACTION OF VIOLET FIRE in, through and around every electron that makes up the atoms of my emotional, mental, etheric and physical vehicles, until they outpicture the God Perfection which Thou art!

(Repeat 3 times)

In the Name of the Almighty Presence of God "I AM" and the Holy Christ Self pulsating in every human heart...

SATURATE MY FEELING WORLD WITH THE VIOLET TRANSMUTING FLAME (3 times)

SATURATE MY MENTAL WORLD WITH THE VIO-
LET TRANSMUTING FLAME (3 times)
SATURATE MY ETHERIC WORLD WITH THE VIO-
LET TRANSMUTING FLAME (3 times)
SATURATE MY PHYSICAL WORLD WITH THE
VIOLET TRANSMUTING FLAME (3 times)

In God's Most Holy Name "I AM".

8. *Visualization for Transmuting the Past Through
the Violet Flame of Forgiveness*

Sit or lie down comfortably with your arms and legs
uncrossed. Breathe in deeply, and as you exhale, completely relax and feel all of the tension just drop away.
Gently close your eyes and visualize yourself in a
beautiful relaxing place...lying in the warm Sun on a
soothing beach or resting on the soft green grass in a
peaceful meadow. Feel the warmth of the Sun, as you
feel safe and secure. With each breath you become
more and more relaxed, more calm and serene.

As you are relaxing under the Sun, see yourself within
a forcefield of peace and protection. Then, you see a
circle beginning to form around you. You ask your
Holy Christ Self to bring into the circle every experience
that is blocking your transformation, every experience
that is keeping you bound and stuck in limitation. In
the circle, you will find experiences of past hate and
anger. There will be feelings of jealousy, fear, envy
and doubt.

You begin to see experiences from the past that caused
you pain, hurt and sadness. You see experiences that
made you feel bad about yourself, experiences that
made you feel worthless, not valuable, unimportant.
You see experiences that robbed you of your dignity,
your self-respect, your self-esteem.

You begin to realize that you are bound to these experiences, these people and these events from the
past by ropes. You are not creating the ropes; you are
merely recognizing that they are already there,

created in the past through negative feelings and thoughts.

All of these experiences, and the people involved in them, are bound to you by ropes. Any other experience that you have ever had that is preventing you from achieving limitless physical perfection or is preventing you from being transformed into the perfection of your Holy Christ Self also begins forming in the circle.

Now, to FREE yourself from the past, and to FREE yourself from these limiting conditions, you call forth, through the Power of God anchored in your heart, the VIOLET TRANSMUTING FLAME.

This sacred essence begins to pour into your heart, and you project it forth from your heart into the circle, filling the entire circle with the full gathered momentum of *mercy, compassion, forgiveness, transmutation, justice, opportunity* and *freedom*. The Violet Flame blazes in, through and around every electron of energy within the circle. It becomes radiant and glows. It begins to transmute and burn through the ropes.

Feel this crystalline Violet Flame FREEING you from all of this negative energy and FREEING those in the circle as well. Feel It blazing higher and higher, as It burns through the ropes, dissolving all the negativity.

As the healing takes place through the Law of Forgiveness, you begin to experience liberation and freedom. Now, you forgive yourself and others for their negative behavior toward you, and yours toward them as you affirm:

Law of Forgiveness

With all the power of the Beloved Presence of God "I AM", and the Violet Ray of eternal love, mercy, compassion and transmutation...

I FORGIVE! I FORGIVE! I FORGIVE!

every person, place, condition or thing that may have wronged me in any way, at any time, for any reason whatsoever, and I now LOVE FREE all debts owed to me by life everywhere.

I do now invoke the Law of Forgiveness for myself and all Humanity, for all misuse of God's Holy Energy since the beginning of time.

FORGIVE ME! FORGIVE ME! FORGIVE ME!

and as I am forgiven, I send forth a gift of love to balance all debts to life I have ever created which yet remain unpaid.

"I AM" grateful for the Law of Forgiveness. "I AM" loving life free from the Wheel of Cause and Effect before it can act, manifest or longer be sustained.

IT IS DONE! AS "I AM" GOD IN ACTION. SO BE IT!

See, feel and know the Violet Transmuting Flame is burning through the ropes. It is a beautiful feeling to know that whatever it was in the past that prevented you from recognizing your true God reality is now leaving you once and for all. As you are released from the limitations, you radiate out into the circle the pink essence of your love. You also radiate pink love out to everyone in your family, your friends and loved ones, until your LOVE is literally flooding the Planet.

Love and acceptance flows through you to all life. You are FREE, and they are FREE too. You then seal this activity of Light and affirm:

I AM FREE! I AM FREE! I AM ETERNALLY FREE!
I ASK MY GOD PRESENCE TO SUSTAIN THIS
ACTIVITY THROUGH ME, INCREASING IT WITH
EVERY BREATH I TAKE.

Feeling the buoyancy and joy of this new found FREEDOM, gently return your attention to the room. Become aware of your physical body, breathe in deeply, and as you exhale, gently open your eyes.

9. *Visualization to Experience the Seven Chakra Centers Being Reborn Into the Twelve Chakra Centers*
In this exercise, we will experience the physical spine of our Holy Christ Self being brought into alignment with the spiritual spine of our "I AM" Presence.

Begin by standing straight with your feet a few inches apart. Now, feel the flow of Sacred Fire Ascending from the root chakra at the base of the spine up the spinal column into your crown chakra at the top of your head and back down to the root chakra again. This Sacred Fire is a spiralling forcefield of your Father-Mother God, a Blue Flame reflecting the Masculine Polarity of God, and a Pink Flame, reflecting the Feminine Polarity of God, spiralling up and down your spine in a great dance of radiant Light. Breathe slowly and rhythmically. Clear your mind of all thoughts and concentrate on this sacred activity of spiritual evolution.

(Pause)

The Masculine and Feminine Flames now spiral in perfect balance and harmony, performing their dance of Light as the Universal Life Force courses through your four planetary bodies (physical, etheric, mental and emotional). FEEL the seven planetary chakras, each reflecting the perfection of the Holy Christ Self and the completion of its purpose. Feel each planetary chakra in perfect balance, reflecting its Masculine/Feminine Aspects in absolute harmony.

Root Chakra – Red
Central Chakra – Orange
Solar Plexus Chakra – Yellow
Heart Chakra – Green
Throat Chakra – Blue
Third Eye Chakra – Indigo
Crown Chakra – Violet

When the Sacred Fires of your Father-Mother God are in perfect balance within your four lower vehicles, you begin to experience a moment of rapid absorption into the greater vibration of your "I AM" Presence. Instantaneously, but very gently, you feel the great rod of Solar Fire blazing with Twelve Solar Chakras along your spine. These Twelve Solar Chakras are like blazing Suns, and reflect the perfection of each of the Twelve Aspects of Deity.

At the base of the Solar Spine is the White Aspect of Purity. Next, the Opal Aspect of Transformation. Then:

the Violet Aspect of Freedom,
the Ruby Aspect of Ministering Grace,
the Peach Aspect of Divine Purpose,
the Gold Aspect of Peace,
the Pink Aspect of Divine Love,
the Magenta Aspect of Harmony,
the Blue Aspect of God's Will,
the Aquamarine Aspect of Clarity,
the Green Aspect of Truth,
the Yellow Aspect of Enlightenment

(See illustration page 153).

The lesser planetary spine is absorbed into the greater Solar Spine; the planetary identity becomes the heightened identity of a God Being. This greater identity is an electronic pattern of free flowing Light rather than the atomic pattern of fixed proportions of atoms and molecules you have accepted as being your physical identity on the material plane. It is this electronic pattern of your Divine identity that literally dances with the Light of the Sun. Like a celestial gem, Its aura captures a spectacular aureole of Solar Radiance, Cosmic Colors and Divine Qualities. It is this electronic pattern of Celestial Light that is your permanent identity. It is this electronic pattern that assimilates the totality of God's Perfection and continually radiates those Divine blessings forth to all life.

As you accept and know your Divine identity, affirm with deep feeling:

"I AM" the Eternal Flame of Life...a White Fire Being from the Heart of the Almighty.
I dwell within my Twelve-fold Ray from out of the Great Central Sun...crowned with the Twelve Diamond Rays of Attainment.
I abide upon my Sacred Lotus Throne of Light...letting my Love flow out to all Creation.
"I AM" a Sun in the Infinite Palace of Light...my world the Altar of Infinite Space...my Radiance...the Peace of the Great Solar Quiet.
"I AM" the undying Flame of Life everywhere, the Great Eternal Joy, Glory, Perfection of Existence.
"I AM"..."I AM"..."I AM"...Twelve times Twelve "I AM".
I wear pure golden sandals with ribbons of Light, a Crown made of Sun Rays, a Cloak of God Might. I carry a Scepter, my focus of Power. I pour forth Pure Christ Light each moment...each hour.

Group Avatar

10. *The Supreme Initiation into Christhood*

The Supreme Initiation has been revealed to Humanity as a merciful act of Divine Love. This Initiation is specifically designed to awaken the Elemental vortexes within our four lower bodies. The process will raise the vibration of each of our four vehicles back into the Light Body of our Holy Christ Selves.

The Elemental vortexes will then sustain the limitless physical perfection of our four lower bodies as was originally intended. We must accept this Sacred Knowledge with deep humility and reverence and use it ONLY as directed, knowing full well that, if this truth is used to perpetuate the human ego or for self-aggrandizement, the Law of the Circle will be instantaneous and just.

Before we begin this Initiation, we must be prepared to make changes in our lives. The radiant Light of our Holy Christ Self will clearly expose the illusions and deceptions of our distorted belief systems. We must ask ourselves before beginning:

AM I READY TO OPEN MYSELF TO THE BLAZING REALMS OF ILLUMINED TRUTH?

AM I READY TO BECOME ONE WITH THE PRESENCE OF GOD PULSATING IN MY HEART?

AM I READY TO TRANSFORM MY LIFE AND MY PHYSICAL REALITY?

If the answer to all of these questions is YES, from the innermost part of your being, *then and only then*, may you proceed.

The Supreme Initiation

All that exists in the Universe is the vibration of many spectrums of Living Light. Vibration is actually the Law of the Universe, and all life breathes and expresses the essential nature of vibration through rhythm.

In order to attune ourselves with the vibration and rhythm of the Universe, it is essential that we master the technique of the Balanced Breath. Our ability to reach up in vibration into our God Presence is based upon the foundation of the Balanced Breath.

If we open our minds to the existence of Pranic Energy, the Breath of the Holy Spirit, we will become aware of Its Presence. With every breath, we absorb this vital force of life, and we depend on it to remain healthy and alive. Within our Holy Christ Selves there are specialized centers that serve as forcefields to magnetize and radiate forth this Holy Essence into our four lower bodies. These centers are seen as swirling vortexes of concentrated Light, and they are separate from the chakra system. These centers vibrate at a higher frequency than our four lower bodies, and they are associated with the five Elements: ether (Spirit), air, fire, water and earth.

These five Elemental vortexes continually magnetize highly spiritualized energy from the Octaves of Perfection. Each center represents a force of Sacred Fire, the Breath of Holy Spirit, and as the centers are activated through the Supreme Initiation, we will experience a transformation in our physical, etheric, mental and emotional bodies at an atomic cellular level. The five Elemental vortexes are receptive forcefields which receive energies from the Holy Spirit on the Holy Breath. This is a Feminine Energy Force that is being activated now as never before to accelerate the Feminine Ray Nature of Balance and Harmony through all life.

The Supreme Initiation is a method whereby the Elemental centers will be deliberately awakened into full vibrant activity according to the Divine Plan of each individual. It is very important that this awakening process be done *slowly* and *thoroughly*.

In order to accomplish the Supreme Initiation, we must continually manifest DIVINE TRUTH in our daily lives. Each of us must go within and earnestly endeavor to practice the Spiritual Truths we are now receiving consciously from the Fourth Dimensional Realms.

The Supreme Initiation is, of course, the initiation into the reality of our true being, our Holy Christ Self. This initiation cannot be accomplished through intellect. It will be attained ONLY through the perpetual practice of the Presence of God.

The veil has been lifted, and now through our open hearts, our invocation of the Light and our reverence for all life, we shall BECOME God Illumination on Earth–the Christ.

The transformation taking place is occurring at an atomic cellular level. Consequently, through the five Elements comprising all manifest form, we shall pass through the steps of the Supreme Initiation into Christhood.

Through this Sacred Initiation, each of us will be victorious over matter. Then, our bodies of Earthly expression will be transformed into Light. We will then be "in the world, but not of it." We will be the Christ, grown to full stature, manifesting Celestial lives of beauty and harmony in every single facet. Then, we will affirm with a KNOWING beyond the comprehension of our finite minds:

> "I AM" a Sun/Son...My love Its Light.
> "I AM" a force of God moving upon this Planet.
> "I AM" ONE with all Light, the Great Universal Consciousness.
> "I AM" that "I AM".

STEP ONE
THE BALANCED BREATH

To begin the exercise, we sit comfortably with our spines as straight as possible, and our bodies relaxed. We concentrate on our breathing, gently counting in our minds the length of the IN breath and the length of the OUT breath. We then calmly adjust the inbreath and the outbreath to equal duration.

When we reach this calm, Balanced Breath, we begin to experience ourselves becoming aligned with the harmony of the Universe. After a few minutes of Balanced Breathing, we begin to *feel* a force of subtle vitality growing and spreading through our bodies. This is Pranic Energy or the Breath of the Holy Spirit. This Holy Breath is the vital life-sustaining essence that permeates and sustains all life. We are not to force the conscious control of the breath, but just relax and practice this technique of Balanced Breathing until we perceive a definite sensation. As we do, we begin to accept and know that the breath is the most essential process of life.

Only after we *FEEL* the vitality of the Holy Breath through the practice of Balanced Breathing are we ready to proceed to the next step.

STEP TWO OF THE SUPREME INITIATION
The Ether/Spirit Vortex

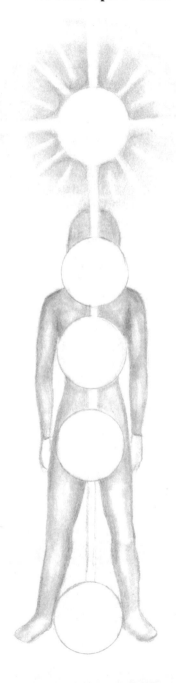

STEP TWO
THE ETHER/SPIRIT VORTEX

Step two of the Supreme Initiation: We are enveloped now in a forcefield of protection and comfort. We are at peace! We are centered! We are one with all life!

In this harmonious state we begin to feel the vital Life Force of the Holy Spirit flowing through our beings. This essence lifts us into a heightened state of awareness.

Now, we concentrate our entire consciousness on the Three-fold Flame in our hearts—the true center of our beings. As this occurs, all of our senses are focused inward as each breath penetrates deeper and deeper into the Divinity within.

When we feel completely centered in our own Divinity, we move our focus of attention upward. It rises slowly until we reach a point twelve inches above our heads. There, we perceive a point of brilliant vibrating White Light. With the full power of our Divinity we affirm into the center point of Light:

"I AM" THAT "I AM"

On each inbreath we affirm "I AM" that "I AM" into the Ether/Spirit Center above our heads, and on each outbreath, we visualize that center point of Light awakening into a blazing Sun. As it grows, it gathers intensity and momentum, becoming a rotating, pulsating vortex of Light.

As we continue to silently intone the affirmation into the Ether/Spirit Vortex, we feel the effects of the awakening spiritual energy emanating into our consiousness, flooding our beings with pure life vitality.

This experience is powerful and intense. We are actually awakening to the center of pure spiritual intelligence within us. Every cell and atom of our bodies is affected and responds. From our new heightened awareness our view of reality begins to change. We release our attachments to the world of illusion, and we gradually perceive the perfection of God's Will through the chaos.

During this period of awakening the Ether/Spirit Vortex, we will realize we are activating a part of our beings that has been dormant. This process causes a flood of pure Light to enter our consciousness.

To completely activate this center, we must continue this exercise for a *MINIMUM OF FIFTEEN MINUTES EVERY DAY FOR SEVEN DAYS*. It is extremely important that we awaken the center fully and completely.

The Divine Plan for all creation is for the perfection of the Immaculate Concept to reflect on the physical planes of matter. Through this process, physical matter Ascends into the Divine Blueprint.

THE LIGHT BODY–ETHER/SPIRIT

Through the above exercise, the Spiritual Light Body is activated, and if we will continually contemplate and apply the following guidelines, this step of the Supreme Initiation will be fulfilled.

GUIDELINES TO MY PERFECTION

1. "I Am" renewing my mind.
2. "I Am" lifting up my vision to see myself as God sees me–radiantly healthy and filled with joy and peace.
3. "I Am" whole, perfect and complete.
4. "I Am" meditating daily on my Divine Image.
5. I go about my business with an uplifted consciousness of health and well-being.
6. I live the TRUTH of health.
7. "I Am" reprogramming my consciousness on a mental level. "I Am" also continuing my health work in the physical world of form.
8. My thoughts and actions are harmonious and balanced.
9. I eat and exercise properly and affirm perfect health, knowing the health of my body reflects my mind. It is the physical image of my mental atmosphere.
10. "I Am" aware of the total interrelationship of mind, body and Spirit in creating a state of well-being in myself.
11. My God Presence perceives only perfection in me. It is the Will of God in individual expression.
12. "I Am" seeing my four lower bodies–physical, etheric, mental and emotional as my God Presence sees them–perfect and raised into my LIGHT BODY. My life is God's Life, and God's Life is perfect.

STEP THREE OF THE SUPREME INITIATION
The Air Vortex

STEP THREE

After completing seven consecutive days of activating the Ether/Spirit Vortex for a minimum of fifteen minutes each day, we are ready to proceed to the next step.

The Supreme Initiation is *always* done in ordered sequence, so step three begins by repeating step one and two for a few minutes. After silently intoning "I AM" that "I AM" into the Ether/Spirit Vortex for a few minutes, we visualize a shaft of pure, white, radiant Light flowing down from the sphere above our heads to a point of blazing white Light in our throat centers. We feel the inrush of Light through this shaft activate the point of Light until it, too, begins to expand into a brilliant rotating Sun.

With the full gathered momentum of our Divinity, we silently intone into the Air Vortex awakening in our throats the affirmation:

"I AM" THE BREATH OF THE HOLY SPIRIT

On each inbreath, we intone the affirmation into the Air Vortex, and on each outbreath, we experience the sphere awakening into a blazing Sun.

This center must also be activated for at least fifteen minutes every day for seven consecutive days. During our sojourn within the Air Vortex, we will be lifted higher in consciousness, and our ability to express ourselves clearly will be enhanced. We will discover new ways to communicate, and we will be able to alleviate much of our past inappropriate verbiage. Our old belief systems that no longer apply to our present state of growth will also come into view, giving us the opportunity to release them and replace them with our new found insight.

THE ETHERIC BODY–AIR

Through the activation of the Air Vortex, our etheric bodies are lifted into our Light Bodies. If we contemplate and apply these guidelines, step three of the Supreme Initiation will be fulfilled.

THE PURIFICATION OF
MY RECORDS AND MEMORIES OF THE PAST.

1. "I Am" Purifying my subconscious mind–every experience of the past–transmuting it–cause, core, effect, record and memory into Light.
2. My Etheric Body is spiritually pure. "I Am" free of the world of illusion.
3. "I Am" reaching into the Octaves of Truth and breathing in the Holy Breath of God.
4. I invoke the Light of clarity to shine on the records of the past and lift them into the Light of understanding.
5. "I Am" developing the qualities of Divine Expression, Perception and Discernment.
6. "I Am" passing through the truth of discernment from the world of illusion into the Light of reality.
7. "I Am" balance.
8. "I Am" accepting my true God reality.
9. "I Am" a focus of radiant, positive thoughts filled with gentleness and compassion.
10. My life is a manifestation of my past thoughts. "I Am" changing my thoughts to be one with Divine Will. Therefore, "I Am" changing my life.

STEP FOUR OF THE SUPREME INITIATION
The Fire Vortex

STEP FOUR

After completing seven consecutive days of activating the Air Vortex for a minimum of fifteen minutes each day, we are ready to proceed to the next step.

We begin by repeating steps one, two and three for a few minutes. When the spiritual energy in the throat reaches its full intensity, we visualize another shaft of pure white Light flowing down until it reaches a point of Light pulsating at the base of our sternum in the center of our chests. As the Fire Vortex becomes activated, it begins to rotate and expand into a radiant Sun. With the full momentum of our Divinity, we silently intone into the Fire Vortex the affirmation:

"I AM" THE FIRE BREATH OF THE ALMIGHTY

On each inbreath, we silently intone the affirmation into the Fire Vortex, and on each outbreath, we visualize the sphere awakening into a blazing Sun.

As the sphere expands, we feel the warmth glowing and growing. The vibrations of love touch our hearts, and we feel more complete, centered and whole than ever before. The Divine Flame is a wonderous gift from our God Presence.

While activating the Fire Vortex, we become aware of the ways in which our vital energies are utilized daily. We begin to recognize ways in which we are allowing ourselves to be depleted. Through this observation, we will be able to make positive adjustments in the way we expend our life energy. Positive growth requires effort and a will to change. Awareness always creates a responsibility to act on the knowledge gained.

THE MENTAL BODY–FIRE

Through the activation of the Fire Vortex, our mental bodies ascend into our Light Bodies. If we contemplate and apply these guidelines, step four of the Supreme Initiation will be fulfilled.

"I AM" ONE WITH THE DIVINE MIND OF GOD

1. Through the Initiation of Sacred Fire, I realize love is the First Cause of all life.
2. The Initiation of the Sacred Fire reveals my God Presence "I Am".
3. However brilliant the mind, it must reflect the love of God to be fulfilled.
4. The Sacred Fire Initiation brings warmth, Light and beauty to life.
5. In the Fourth Dimension, Sacred Fire creates and gives life.
6. The Sacred Fire Initiation opens a portal to Divinity.
7. Faith, hope and love are governing my thoughts. Faith is an inward knowing that all is working for my highest good. Hope is an ever-growing confidence in God's Wisdom. Love illumines my heart.
8. Through the Sacred Fire Initiation, I have the power to illuminate the world.
9. The life and love of God are my true reality.
10. The Divine Mind of God floods my being and enhances all my creative power.
11. Love transforms life, removing all that is unwanted, lifting each Lifestream into the perfection of the God Presence "I Am."

STEP FIVE OF THE SUPREME INITIATION
The Water Vortex

STEP FIVE

After completing seven consecutive days of activating the Fire Vortex for a minimum of fifteen minutes each day, we are ready to proceed to the next step.

We begin by repeating steps one, two, three and four for a few minutes. When the Fire Vortex has reached its optimum expansion, we visualize another shaft of pure white Light descending down until it reaches a point of Light vibrating at the base of our spinal column. As the shaft of Light penetrates into this seed point of Light, it begins to awaken the Water Vortex into a blazing Sun. With the full momentum of our Divinity, we silently intone into the Water Sphere the affirmation:

"I AM" THE HARMONY OF MY TRUE BEING

On each inbreath, we silently intone the affirmation into the Water Vortex, and on each outbreath, we experience the sphere expanding into a vibrant Sun.

The Water Vortex is associated with the emotional body, and it is often the most challenging center to awaken in the Supreme Initiation. Suppressed emotional energy rises to the surface to be transmuted into Light during this step of the Initiation. The suppressed emotional patterns are a result of our distorted perceptions and programming from the past. These are the feelings and beliefs that have been keeping us struck in the past and blocked from moving forward into our highest potential.

THE EMOTIONAL BODY–WATER

Through the activation of the Water Sphere, our emotional bodies are raised into our Light Bodies. Through the contemplation and application of these guidelines, step five of the Supreme Initiation will be fulfilled.

1. Be STILL and know that "I AM" God.
2. I have transmuted all my emotions into harmony by giving my God Presence dominion.
3. "I Am" gently leading my feelings and emotions into God's garden of harmony and balance.
4. "I Am" continually utilizing the God Qualities of Discernment and Discrimination.
5. I nurture my emotions with humility and simplicity.
6. "I Am" determined to live truth from my innermost being.
7. My emotions are disciplined to be tranquil and patient.
8. "I Am" always calm enough to reflect the vision and voice of God.
9. "I Am" perpetually a manifest expression of spiritual truth.
10. I recognize my challenges and responsibilities as opportunities for growth, and I experience them with joy.
11. I realize the Love, Wisdom and Power of God, therefore "I Am" experiencing a spiritual life filled with light, freedom and Divine Purpose.
12. "I Am" the illumined consciousness of tranquility and peace.
13. I anoint my being with the knowledge of God, and "I Am" serenity.
14. "I Am" cleansing and purifying my emotional body with the Violet Transmuting Flame of Love.
15. "I Am" focused on the harmony and balance of the Christ within.
16. I seek only God.

EXERCISE TO RESTORE BALANCE

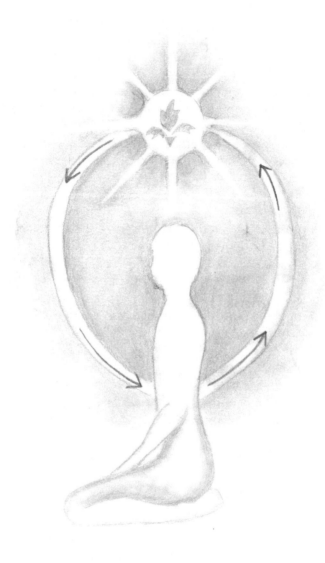

As the Light of God pours through our beings, It enters the electronic substance of our four lower bodies at a cellular level, thus pushing all of the frequencies of discord to the surface to be transmuted at an accelerated pace. This often causes discomfort and some imbalance in our lives. We must acknowledge that we are NEVER given anything we can't withstand, so it is important for us not to stop the process. There is, however, an exercise that will alleviate the discomfort and help restore balance, as the purification is taking place. Remember always, that once this process is truly complete, we will never again be prisoners of our painful past. We will be FREE to magnetize the incomprehensible joy of the Fourth Dimension into our lives. We will then experience the fulfillment of the invocation, "Thy Kindgom come, Thy will be done on Earth as it is in Heaven."

To begin the exercise, we sit comfortably in a chair and attain the Balanced Breath. Once we have experienced a definite sensation of heightened awareness, we visualize an intense Three-fold Flame blazing above our heads within the Ether/Spirit Vortex. As we breathe out, we send a stream of "The Fire Breath of the Almighty" in an arc from the Ether/Spirit Vortex around the front of our bodies into the Solar Plexus just above the navel. This is the spot in our bodies where our emotional energies are most intensely felt. As we breathe in the stream of Light, "The Fire Breath of the Almighty" radiates through our four lower bodies, absorbing every discordant frequency of vibration. The Flame then passes out our backs and arcs back up into the Three-fold Flame blazing in the Ether/Spirit Vortex where the discordant frequencies are instantly transmuted into Light. Again on the outbreath, "The Fire Breath of the Almighty" arcs around our bodies into the Solar Plexus. On the inbreath, it passes out our backs having absorbed all discordant frequencies of vibration and carries them into the Three-fold Flame in the Ether/Spirit Vortex for instant transmutation.

This is a very simple, but extremely powerful exercise, and we should continue to do it until the discomfort is dissipated and the balance restored.

I advise you again to follow the directions for the Supreme

Initiation EXACTLY. It's important that we not become impatient and rush ahead. We have been waiting aeons of time for these Sacred Truths to be revealed to us. They have been held in abeyance because the Heavenly Host felt our consciousness was not raised sufficiently to enable us to use them correctly and safely. We are now being trusted with these Sacred Truths. Let's prove that we are indeed trustworthy. Discipline is the key to Self-Mastery.

The Water Vortex must also be activated for fifteen minutes a day for seven consecutive days before proceeding to the next step of the Supreme Initiation, which is the activation of the Earth Vortex.

STEP SIX OF THE SUPREME INITIATION
The Earth Vortex

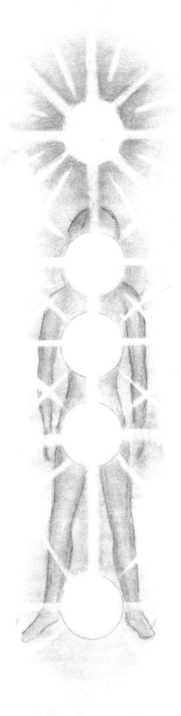

STEP SIX

After repeating steps one, two, three, four and five of the Supreme Initiation for a few minutes, we experience a cascading shaft of pure white Light pouring down from the Water Vortex to a point of Light situated between our feet. The Light begins to illuminate the Earth Vortex as it becomes a brilliant rotating Sun.

Into the point of Light between our feet, we silently intone with our full Divinity, the affirmation:

"I AM" THE MASTER OF MY PHYSICAL REALITY

On the inbreath, we intone the affirmation; on the outbreath, we visualize the Earth Vortex expanding into a brilliant Sun.

As the Earth Vortex is activated, we become a living, shining pillar of Light, a pure white radiant pathway of Light, linking all of our Elemental Vortexes from head to foot.

The awakening of the Earth Vortex will be experienced by each of us as a tremendous relief, for we will now feel balanced in every respect. The major areas of our lives that will arise during the activation of the Earth Vortex will be our physical, material realities. Our entire physical world will be surfacing for evaluation and adjustment. Physical possessions, attachments, care of our physical bodies and material needs will all be brought under scrutiny.

Through the Earth Initiation, we will learn how to effectively use the creative faculties of thought and feeling to project Divine Will onto physical energy (matter), thus creating perfection on Earth.

THE PHYSICAL BODY–EARTH

Now, with the activation of the Earth Vortex, our physical bodies are raised into our Light Bodies. The fulfillment of step six of the Supreme Initiation will be accomplished through the contemplation and application of the following guidelines:

1. "I Am" aware that all energy originally came from God. Everything which seems like solid matter is, in reality, charged with Divine Energy and Light.
2. "I Am" free from matter through the realization that all life is One and responds instantly to the quality of Divine

Love.

3. My physical body is healed and protected through my invocation of God's Will and Protection.

4. "I Am" going within to the Divine Flame in my heart. Through this activity, the atomic structure of my physical body, at a cellular level, is refined and filled with Light. My body is etherealized. "I Am" residing in a body of Light while still in the physical world. *"I AM" IN THE WORLD, BUT NOT OF IT.*

5. The Divine Flame in my heart calls forth the love vibration within every electron of my Being, awakening each one to the voice of my God Presence "I Am".

6. Through the Earth Initiation, "I Am" lifted into the awareness that the purpose of my Earthly existence is to acknowledge and accept my power of command over the five elements and all physical matter, thus becoming master of my physical reality.

7. I Invoke the Ray of God's Love into every electron of my being and into every electron on Earth. My body and consciousness and that of all Humanity is NOW accepting the original Divine Plan of Perfection that has always been known in the Fourth Dimension.

8. Within every electron of the bodies of Humanity and the Elemental Kingdom, I FEEL the Cosmic Nature of Divine Love. Through this Divine Love, anything not of the Light is being transmuted into God's Perfection.

9. "I AM" now seeing and feeling the original crystal clarity of every electron of precious life energy evolving on Earth. Within this crystal clarity is held the Immaculate Concept of all physical matter.

10. Within the balance of the Masculine and Feminine Polarity of God, an indisputable aura of Divine Love has formed on Earth, and the Christ within the hearts of all Humanity is being called forth.

11. Humanity! Planet Earth! Awake! Step forth into the Fourth Dimension of Unconditional Love and *BE* the perfection of your true God reality on Earth.

To bring the activation of the Earth Vortex to fulfillment, the exercise must be done for a minimum of fifteen minutes each day for seven consecutive days.

STEP SEVEN OF THE SUPREME INITIATION
Directing the Light Force

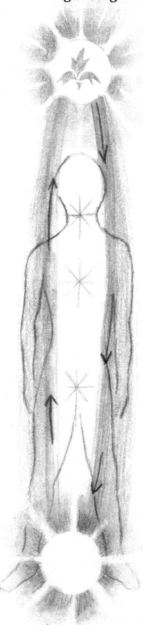

PINK
"AM"

BLUE
"I"

**BALANCING THE
MASCULINE AND FEMININE
POLARITIES OF GOD**

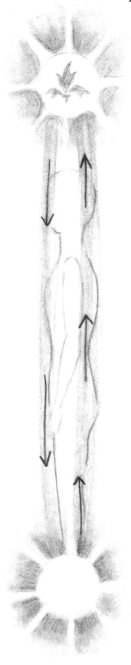

YELLOW/GOLD
*"I AM" the Christ
Grown to Full Stature!*

**BATHING THE
BODY IN PURE
CHRIST LIGHT**

STEP SEVEN

Now that we have activated the five Elemental Vortexes within our four lower bodies creating a tremendous pathway of radiant Light through our beings from head to toe, we are ready to utilize this powerful and dynamic force to quicken the evolution of our consciousness and that of all life on Earth. We are NOW an activated Light Body of God's Perfection, and through the conscious direction of this energy, we can assist in healing the minds, bodies and emotions of all life evolving on this Planet. The Supreme Initiation, therefore, enables us to elevate our powers of service to our fellow beings on Earth.

To begin attaining this greater power, we must learn how to consciously direct this potent Light Force. To start the process, we stand and quickly pass through the six preceeding steps of the Supreme Initiation. After completing the Earth Vortex, we feel the Energy ascending from the Earth Vortex up the pathway of Light into the Ether/Spirit Vortex above our heads. Within the Ether/Spirit Vortex we see and feel the blazing Three-fold Flame of God. Pulsating to the right is the Pink Flame of Divine Love representing the Feminine Aspect of God—Holy Spirit/Divine Mother Principle. Pulsating to the left is the Blue Flame of God's Will representing the Masculine Aspect of God—the Father. Rising up from the center is the Yellow/Gold Flame representing the Son/Daughter Principle of God—the Christ/Wisdom. Now, as we breathe out, we feel the vibrant Blue Flame of God's Will flowing down from the Ether/Spirit Vortex above our heads, through the left side of our bodies down to the Earth Vortex between our feet. Then as we breathe in, we feel the crystalline Pink Flame of pure Divine Love rising up through the right side of our bodies from the Earth Vortex into the Pink Flame pulsating on the right side of the Ether/Spirit Vortex. On the outbreath, the Blue Flame of Divine Will flows through the left side of the body from the Ether/Spirit Vortex down to the Earth Vortex. On the inbreath, the Pink Flame of Divine Love ascends up the right side of the body from the Earth Vortex into the Ether/Spirit Vortex. This breath, designed to balance the Masculine and Feminine Polarities of God within us, is continued for at least five minutes.

Then, while still standing, we focus our attention on the Yellow/Gold Flame of the Christ/Wisdom in the Ether/Spirit Vortex. On the outbreath, we consciously direct the Golden Light of Christ from the Ether/Spirit Vortex down the front of our bodies to the Earth Vortex between our feet. On the inbreath, we magnetize the Golden Christ Light up the back of our bodies from the Earth Vortex to the Ether/Spirit Vortex above our heads. As we breathe out, the Christ Light descends, bathing the front of our bodies. As we breathe in, the Christ Light ascends, bathing the back of our bodies. This process is also continued for at least five minutes.

STEP EIGHT OF THE SUPREME INITIATION
Directing the Twelve-Fold Aspect of Deity
from the Fifth Dimension

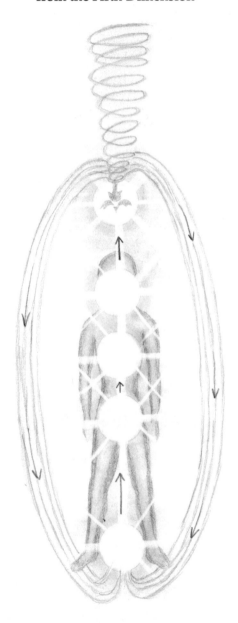

STEP EIGHT

After doing step seven of the Supreme Initiation, "Directing the Light Force," for ten minutes a day for seven consecutive days, we are ready for the eighth and final step of the Supreme Initiation. Through this exercise, we will magnetize into our beings and the atmosphere of Earth, the highest frequency of vibration this Earth has ever experienced. It is a frequency of the Twelve-fold Aspect of Deity from the Cosmic Holy Spirit in the Fifth Dimension. It is known as "The Fire Breath of the Almighty."

To begin this process we stand and pass quickly through steps one through seven of the Supreme Initiation. Then we witness, pouring into our Ether/Spirit Vortex from a focus of the Cosmic Holy Spirit in the Fifth Dimension, a spiralling forcefield of Light blazing with the multi-colored Rays of the Twelve-fold Aspect of Deity. This spiralling shaft of Light is securely anchored in the Three-fold Flame within our Ether/Spirit Vortex. Now, as we breathe out, a cascading fountain of the Twelve-fold Aspect of Deity is projected from our Ether/Spirit Vortex in a profusion of glorious color in every direction in, through and around every electron of our bodies down to the Earth Vortex between our feet. On the inbreath, this Twelve-fold radiance of Light ascends up the center of our beings through the Elemental Vortexes into the Ether/Spirit Vortex above our heads. Again, on the outbreath, a fountain of cascading color radiates out from the Ether/Spirit Vortex through every electron of our beings into the Earth Vortex between our feet. Then, it is breathed up the center of our beings into the Ether/Spirit Vortex again. This sacred activity should be repeated for at least five minutes every day.

It is through the consistent practice of this Supreme Initiation that our evolutionary growth will be greatly accelerated. With the perpetual discipline, we will create a vehicle through which our consciousness can transcend the physical world of form and the wheel of life and death forever.

It is the pathway to the Ascension.

TRANSFORMING THE FOUR LOWER BODIES INTO THE IMMACULATE CONCEPT OF THE HOLY CHRIST SELF

This activity is dedicated to re-establishing the Divine Blueprint...the Immaculate Concept...within your physical, etheric, mental and emotional vehicles.

Through this exercise, you will energize each vehicle until the pulsating force of the Holy Christ Self is within that vehicle, thus regenerating health, beauty, eternal youth and order physically, etherically, mentally and emotionally.

To begin...sit comfortably in a chair with your arms and legs uncrossed and your spine as straight as possible. Breathe in deeply, and as you exhale, completely relax and gently close your eyes. Feel yourself enveloped in an invincible Forcefield of Protection which prevents anything not of the Light from interfering with this sacred activity. This is a journey in consciousness that will physically manifest through the power of your true God reality "I AM".

In projected consciousness, visualize yourself standing before a magnificent Crystaline Temple of Healing in the Realms of Illumined Truth. You ascend the steps and pass through the massive doors. You pass through the alabaster hallway and enter the sacred, central chamber. As you stand within the central chamber, you notice that there are four surrounding chambers at the cardinal points. Pulsating in the center of the central chamber is a radiant crystal Lotus Blossom, and blazing within the center of the Lotus Blossom is a crystalline Madonna Blue Flame with a White aura. It is the Flame of the Immaculate Concept.

An Angelic Being beckons you, and you enter the crystalline Lotus Blossom and stand within the scintillating essence of the Flame of the Immaculate Concept. You begin to experience the vibratory rate of your four lower bodies being accelerated. Your consciousness is rising, and you perceive, more clearly that ever before, the Divine Blueprint for each of your vehicles.

Pouring forth now from the very Heart of God is a tremendous Ray of Light that is pulsating with the God Qualities of Restoration, Transformation, Healing, Eternal Youth and Radiant Beauty. This shaft of Light enters the Flame of the Immaculate Concept, and then expands out to each of the outer chambers at the cardinal points which are dedicated specifically to one of the four lower vehicles of your life's expression.

You now consciously project your emotional body and all of your feelings into the chamber at the cardinal point to the East. God's Holy Light begins blazing in, through and around this vehicle, transmuting every trace of imbalance. Your God Presence now projects the Divine Blueprint for your emotional body through this vehicle, and it begins pulsating as a Light Pattern, transforming this vehicle instantly into the Immaculate Concept of your Holy Christ Self.

You now consciously project your mental body and all of your thoughts into the chamber at the cardinal point to the West. God's Holy Light begins blazing in, through and around this vehicle, transmuting every trace of imbalance. Your God Presence now projects the Divine Blueprint for your mental body through this vehicle, and it begins pulsating as a Light Pattern, transforming this vehicle instantly into the Immaculate Concept of your Holy Christ Self.

You now consciously project your etheric body and all of your memories and records of the past into the chamber at the cardinal point to the North. God's Holy Light begins blazing in, through and around this vehicle, transmuting every trace of imbalance. Your God Presence now projects the Divine Blueprint for your etheric body through this vehicle, and it begins pulsating as a Light Pattern, transforming this vehicle instantly into the Immaculate Concept of your Holy Christ Self.

You now consciously project your physical body, every cell, atom, gland, muscle, organ and function, into the chamber at the cardinal point to the South. God's Holy Light begins blazing in, through and around this vehicle, trans-

SEALING AFFIRMATION

SEALING AFFIRMATION

nPart 1

See Page 219 for Order Form

writing

THE IMMORTAL VICTORIOUS THREE-FOLD FLAME WITHIN THE WHITE FIRE BEING

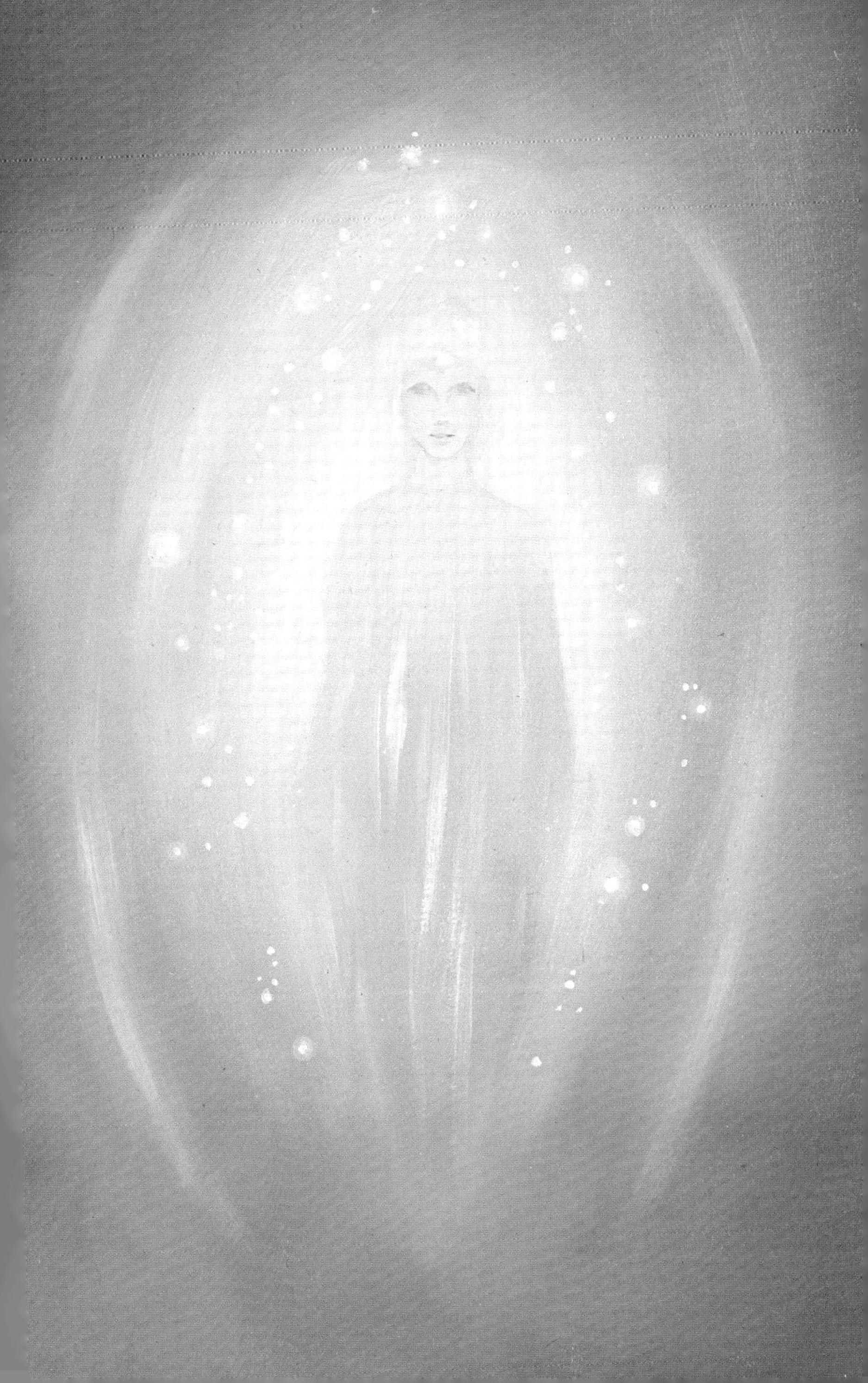

THE "I AM" PRESENCE

THE TWELVE-FOLD CAUSAL BODY
OF THE "I AM" PRESENCE AND
THE TWELVE-FOLD SOLAR SPINE

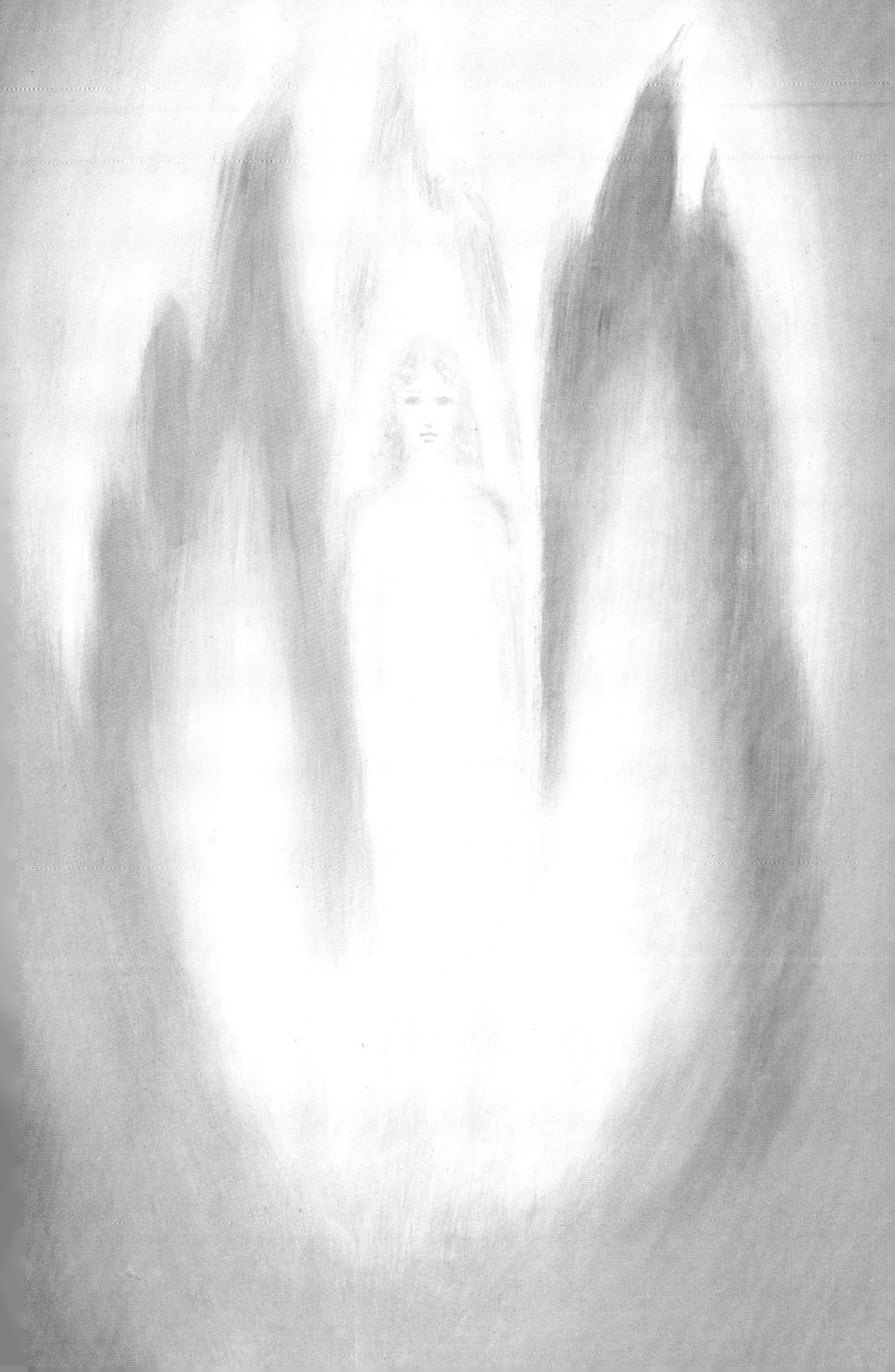

THE HOLY CHRIST SELF ENVELOPED
IN THE IMMORTAL VICTORIOUS
THREE-FOLD FLAME

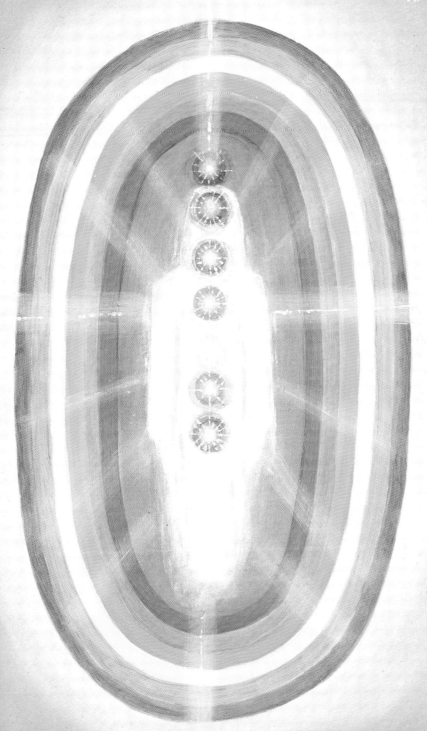

THE SEVEN-FOLD CAUSAL BODY OF THE HOLY CHRIST SELF AND THE SEVEN-FOLD PLANETARY SPINE

THE FOUR LOWER BODIES:
PHYSICAL BODY
ETHERIC BODY (WHITE)
MENTAL BODY (YELLOW)
EMOTIONAL BODY (PINK)
AND THE THREE-FOLD FLAME WITH
THE SILVER CORD

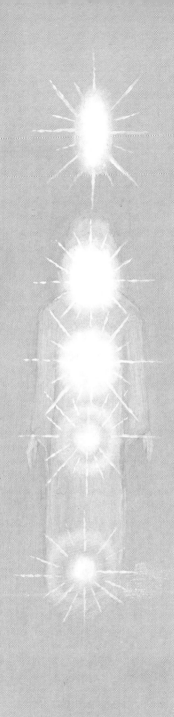

THE FIVE ELEMENTAL VORTEXES:
ETHER/SPIRIT VORTEX (OPAL)
AIR VORTEX/ETHERIC BODY (WHITE)
FIRE VORTEX/MENTAL BODY (YELLOW)
WATER VORTEX/EMOTIONAL BODY (PINK)
EARTH VORTEX/PHYSICAL BODY (GREEN)

TWELVE-FOLD SOLAR SPINE
UNIFYING INTO THE CIRCLE OF THE
SACRED TWELVE AS IT IS STEPPED DOWN
IN FREQUENCY INTO THE
THIRD DIMENSIONAL SEVEN-FOLD
PLANETARY SPINE

155

THE TWELVE SOLAR SUN CYCLES
THE CAUSAL BODY OF GOD

A. SOLAR ASPECT OF DEITY
B. SUN CYCLE AND CORRESPONDING
    CONSTELLATION
C. SOLAR ARCHANGELS AND ARCHAII
D. FOURTH DIMENSIONAL PLANETARY RETREATS
    OF THE SPIRITUAL HIERARCHY
E. HUMANITY'S CHRIST FLAME AT SHAMBALLA
F. GLOBAL GROUP AVATAR'S THREE-FOLD FLAME
G. HUMANITY'S INDIVIDUAL THREE-FOLD FLAME
H. PHYSICAL REALITY – THREE-FOLD FLAME OF
    MOTHER EARTH

(FOR FURTHER DETAILS SEE
CHAPTER THREE, PAGE 158)

CHAPTER
THREE

THE CAUSAL BODY OF GOD

The Causal Body of God, as revealed to Humanity for our present state of evolution, consists of twelve glorious bands of Light known as the twelve Solar Aspects of Deity. These magnificent bands of Light contain within their frequencies the totality of God's Perfection. The Causal Body of God radiates out from the Immortal Victorious Three-fold Flame of God, and It expands to cradle the entire Universe.

Surrounding our particular Solar System, there are twelve constellations that form the natural zodiac. These constellations are Divine Forcefields that magnetize the perfection of the Causal Body of God and project that perfection into the atmosphere of our Solar System in rhythmic pulsations known as Sun Cycles. This Divine Light is absorbed by our physical Sun and rhythmically breathed into Earth on the Holy Breath of our Father-Mother God. Through this process, the Light is gently stepped down into third dimensional frequencies. This occurs as the Earth revolves around our physical Sun in her annual 365¼ day orbit. We can greatly enhance the Divine Light of the twelve Solar Aspects of Deity in our everyday lives if we will consciously be aware of the sacred opportunity presented to us during each Sun Cycle.

The process of projecting the perfection of God's Causal Body into the physical plane of Earth begins by the constellation of the current Sun Cycle, for example, Capricorn, magnetizing the Solar Aspect of Deity from the Causal Body of God and breathing It into the Divine Three-fold Flame of our physical Sun. Our Sun then breathes the perfection of that particular Solar Aspect into Its own Causal Body. Standing within the Twelve-fold Causal Body of our physical Sun are the Mighty Solar Archangels and Their Divine Complements, the twelve Solar Archaii. These glorious Beings absorb the Solar Aspect into Their Three-fold Flames and breathe that Divine Light into the stepped down frequency of the Fourth Dimension. There the Sacred Solar Aspect is absorbed into the Divine Flame that is blazing on the altar of the planetary retreat of the Spiritual Hierarchy that is open during that particular Sun Cycle. The Spiritual Hierarchy of that retreat then breathe the Solar Aspect into the unified forcefield of Humanity's Christ Flame which pulsates on the altar at Shamballa. The Divine Light is then stepped down further into the frequencies of the global Christ Presence of Group Avatar (the Lightworkers). It is then stepped down into the third dimensional frequencies of the Three-fold Flame of the masses of Humanity and finally into the Three-fold Flame of Beloved Mother Earth, thus manifesting as physical reality.

If you will review the chart on page 155 and compare it with the following Sun Cycles, this sacred process of stepping the Causal Body of God down into physical reality will become clearer.

SUN CYCLES CHART
(See Page 155)

A. SOLAR ASPECT OF DEITY
B. SUN CYCLE AND CORRESPONDING CONSTELLATION
C. SOLAR ARCHANGELS AND ARCHAII
D. FOURTH DIMENSIONAL PLANETARY RETREATS OF THE SPIRITUAL HIERARCHY
E. HUMANITY'S CHRIST FLAME AT SHAMBALLA
F. GLOBAL GROUP AVATAR'S THREE-FOLD FLAME
G. HUMANITY'S INDIVIDUAL THREE-FOLD FLAME
H. PHYSICAL REALITY—THREE-FOLD FLAME OF MOTHER EARTH

I.
FIRST SOLAR ASPECT OF DEITY

A. COLOR–BLUE

DIVINE QUALITIES: Divine Will, Illumined Faith, Power, Protection, Decision, the Will to do, Divine Order, Obedience, Intuition, Unity, Discrimination, Discretion, Perception, Victory.

DIVINE INTENT: Majesty... Qualities of knowing "I AM" before all else; thou shalt have no other Gods before Me. Knowing "I AM" Spiritually Free as the very first experience; being totally God. Omnipotent, Omniscient, Omnipresent or "I AM" That "I AM"; infinite Alpha and Omega, First Cause, First Breath; knowing the ALL of everything.

B. SUN CYCLE AND CORRES-
PONDING CONSTELLATION
July 23 through August 22
LEO

C. SOLAR ARCHANGEL AND
ARCHAII FOR THE *FIRST* SOLAR
ASPECT OF DEITY
Archangel Michael
Archaii Faith

D. FOURTH DIMENSIONAL RE-
TREAT OF THE SPIRITUAL
HIERARCHY*
The Etheric Cities of John the Beloved... melding third and Fourth Dimensional aspects of Humanity's existence into one Christ Consciousness, allowing Christ Illumination, Healing and Love Divine to pour forth into every aspect of society's day-to-day life. Hierarch: John the Beloved, Chohan of the Sixth Ray of Perfect Christ Service. Flame: Flame of Ministering Grace.

*(NOTE: The Planetary Retreats change annually with the completion of each 365¼ day planetary orbit around the Sun)

      E. HUMANITY'S CHRIST FLAME
          AT SHAMBALLA

      F. GLOBAL GROUP AVATAR'S
          THREE-FOLD FLAME

      G. HUMANITY'S INDIVIDUAL
          THREE-FOLD FLAME

      H. PHYSICAL REALITY–THE
          THREE-FOLD FLAME OF
          MOTHER EARTH

II.
SECOND SOLAR ASPECT OF DEITY

    A. COLOR–YELLOW

DIVINE QUALITIES: Enlightenment, God Illumination, Wisdom, Understanding, Constancy, Perception, Stimulation and Intensification of Spiritual Growth, A Momentum of Progress, Precipitation, Christ Consciousness.

DIVINE INTENT: Vision of wholeness; focus on Solar reality above all other realities; Divine Immaculate Conception (Divine Concepts); visualization; envisioning limitlessness of the Divine Plan; idealism; Realm of Ideation; clairvoyance; to conceive of all things Immaculately or Divinely.

    B. SUN CYCLE AND CORRES-
       PONDING CONSTELLATION
       June 21 through July 22
       CANCER

C. SOLAR ARCHANGEL AND
ARCHAII FOR THE *SECOND*
SOLAR ASPECT OF DEITY
Archangel Jophiel
Archaii Constance

D. FOURTH DIMENSIONAL RE-
TREAT OF THE SPIRITUAL
HIERARCHY
The Temple of Group Avatar
Consciousness…a focus of Humanity's planetary
Christhood and an acceleration of Humanity's en-
lightenment toward her full responsibility and God
authority for this Planet. Hierarch: The Holy Christ
Selves of all Humanity. Flame: The Three-fold Flame
of Humanity's Christhood at Shamballa.

E. HUMANITY'S CHRIST FLAME
AT SHAMBALLA

F. GLOBAL GROUP AVATAR'S
THREE-FOLD FLAME

G. HUMANITY'S INDIVIDUAL
THREE-FOLD FLAME

H. PHYSICAL REALITY–THE
THREE-FOLD FLAME OF
MOTHER EARTH

III.
THIRD SOLAR ASPECT OF DEITY

A. COLOR–PINK
DIVINE QUALITIES: Divine Love,
Adoration, Tolerance, Humanitarianism, Reverence
for all Life, Balancing the Emotional Body–the Sacred Substance of the Feeling Nature of Humanity.

DIVINE INTENT: Individual God Being within the whole, Divine personalization, knowing "I AM" individually on every plane of existence...differentiation, uniqueness, Divine Identity, Divine Self, evolution into Divine Person.

B. SUN CYCLE AND CORRES-
PONDING CONSTELLATION
May 21 through June 20
GEMINI

C. SOLAR ARCHANGEL AND
ARCHAII FOR THE *THIRD*
SOLAR ASPECT OF DEITY
Archangel Chamuel
Archaii Charity

D. FOURTH DIMENSIONAL RE-
TREAT OF THE SPIRITUAL
HIERARCHY
The Temple of Golden Balance... the Golden Ray of Illumined Love that arises from perfect balance...permeated by the Solar Peace of the Cosmic Christ now radiating into Humanity. Hierarch: Beloved Cosmic Christ. Flame: Solar Three-fold Flame from the Cosmic Christ Focus in the Sun and the Cosmic Christ Planetary Retreat, all focused through the Flame of Humanity's Christ-hood at Shamballa.

E. HUMANITY'S CHRIST FLAME
AT SHAMBALLA

F. GLOBAL GROUP AVATAR'S
THREE-FOLD FLAME

G. HUMANITY'S INDIVIDUAL
THREE-FOLD FLAME

H. PHYSICAL REALITY–THE
THREE-FOLD FLAME OF
MOTHER EARTH

IV.
FOURTH SOLAR ASPECT OF DEITY

A. COLOR–WHITE

DIVINE QUALITIES: Purity, the Immaculate Concept, Hope, Restoration, Resurrection, the Ascension, the Holy Breath, the Sacred Substance of the Mind Nature of Humanity.

DIVINE INTENT: Investiture, empowerment "with the gifts of the Kingdoms," endowment by the Great Universal "I AM", authorized (authority) to act as God, evolution toward being sovereign in the Universe, becoming a God force or forcefield of goodness...stamina, energy, force vitality, potency.

B. SUN CYCLE AND CORRES-
PONDING CONSTELLATION
April 20 through May 20
TAURUS

C. SOLAR ARCHANGEL AND
ARCHAII FOR THE *FOURTH*
SOLAR ASPECT OF DEITY
Archangel Gabriel
Archaii Hope

D. FOURTH DIMENSIONAL RE-
TREAT OF THE SPIRITUAL
HIERARCHY
A Solar and planetary focus of our Beloved Holy Spirit...the Solar Ray of Purity now empowering the tangible Presence of Divine Love to be known within Humanity and the Elemental Kingdom, furthering the reality of limitless physical perfection...the descent of Holy Spirit into Humanity. Hierarch: Beloved Holy AEolus, Cosmic Holy Spirit, the Maha Chohan Paul, planetary Holy Spirit.

Flame: White with a soft Pink Radiance permeating the Planet.

E. HUMANITY'S CHRIST FLAME AT SHAMBALLA

F. GLOBAL GROUP AVATAR'S THREE-FOLD FLAME

G. HUMANITY'S INDIVIDUAL THREE-FOLD FLAME

H. PHYSICAL REALITY–THE THREE-FOLD FLAME OF MOTHER EARTH

V.
FIFTH SOLAR ASPECT OF DEITY

A. COLOR–GREEN

DIVINE QUALITIES: Illumined Truth, Inner Vision, Consecration, Concentration, Healing, Dedication, the All-Seeing Eye of God, the Empowerment of all God Qualities on Earth.

DIVINE INTENT: Wisdom-Truth Divine Mind-Knowing-Becoming, incisive, certainty, confidence, resolve, mindful independence, mindful detachment in serenity, will-power (volition, decision and resoluteness).

B. SUN CYCLE AND CORRESPONDING CONSTELLATION
March 20 through April 19
ARIES

C. SOLAR ARCHANGEL AND
ARCHAII FOR THE *FIFTH*
SOLAR ASPECT OF DEITY
Archangel Raphael
Archaii Mother Mary

D. FOURTH DIMENSIONAL RE-
TREAT OF THE SPIRITUAL
HIERARCHY

The activity of Resurrection and Ascension...taking advantage of the Cosmic currents entering Earth in preparation for Easter and the Resurrection and Ascension of the planetary Christ Presence now to "walk again" amongst Humanity. Hierarch: Beloved Micah, the Angel of Unity re-invigorating Humanity with His own personal Power of Resurrection and Ascension within the flesh vehicle...aided by Beloved Serapis Bey, all the Angels of Resurrection and all the Powers of the Ascension Flame. Flame: Pure White Fire with a Mother of Pearl Radiance and a Violet hue, representing the Flames of Transfiguration, Resurrection and Ascension which were used by Beloved Jesus.

E. HUMANITY'S CHRIST FLAME
AT SHAMBALLA

F. GLOBAL GROUP AVATAR'S
THREE-FOLD FLAME

G. HUMANITY'S INDIVIDUAL
THREE-FOLD FLAME

H. PHYSICAL REALITY–THE
THREE-FOLD FLAME OF
MOTHER EARTH

VI.
SIXTH SOLAR ASPECT OF DEITY

A. COLOR–RUBY

DIVINE QUALITIES: Ministering Grace, Selfless Service, Healing, Devotional Worship, Focus of Love, the Christ-man working through personality, the Divine Image embodied in flesh.

DIVINE INTENT: Holy Spirit, Cosmic Solace...Glorify, Sanctify, Exalt, make Holy, the Blessedness of God "I AM". Grace, Sacredness, Hallowedness, Purity, knowing God's feeling nature and becoming God's feeling nature; stability, knowing the continuity of God in all things; intuitiveness or emotional knowing; emotional wisdom that Love is the God force that keeps all things cohesive, all things in unity, eternity, tranquility, peace, calmness, immutability, changelessness of God, quiescent, equanimity.

B. SUN CYCLE AND CORRES-PONDING CONSTELLATION
February 19 through March 19
PISCES

C. SOLAR ARCHANGEL AND ARCHAII FOR THE *SIXTH* SOLAR ASPECT OF DEITY
Archangel Uriel
Archaii Donna Grace

D. FOURTH DIMENSIONAL RE-TREAT OF THE SPIRITUAL HIERARCHY
The Temple of Consecration to perfect Christ service on Earth. Hierarch: Beloved Archangel Raphael. Flame: A magnificent Green Flame of Consecration...opening in unity with...the Focus of Beloved Mother Mary, holding the Immaculate

Concept of our perfect service, nurturing our perfect "becoming" of a magnificent planetary Christ Presence, just as she did for Beloved Jesus. Hierarch: Beloved Mother Mary, accompanied by Legions of Angels from the Solar and Ascended Master Realms. Flame: A Madonna Blue Flame.

    E. HUMANITY'S CHRIST FLAME AT SHAMBALLA

    F. GLOBAL GROUP AVATAR'S THREE-FOLD FLAME

    G. HUMANITY'S INDIVIDUAL THREE-FOLD FLAME

    H. PHYSICAL REALITY–THE THREE-FOLD FLAME OF MOTHER EARTH

VII.
SEVENTH SOLAR ASPECT OF DEITY

    A. COLOR–VIOLET

    DIVINE QUALITIES: Freedom, Transmutation, Forgiveness, Mercy, Compassion, Rhythm, the Power of Invocation, Divine Justice, Opportunity and Liberty.

    DIVINE INTENT: Transformation, transmutation, acceleration, upshift avataric catalytic. Advancement, progress, to quicken, fission. Synergism: interaction of Divinity, bringing alchemic change or alchemic evolution, harmony.

    B. SUN CYCLE AND CORRESPONDING CONSTELLATION
        January 21 through February 18 AQUARIUS

C. SOLAR ARCHANGEL AND
ARCHAII FOR THE *SEVENTH*
SOLAR ASPECT OF DEITY
Archangel Zadkiel
Archaii Holy Amethyst

D. FOURTH DIMENSIONAL RE-
TREAT OF THE SPIRITUAL
HIERARCHY
A retreat of the Violet Fire, when both the Solar Seventh Ray and planetary Seventh Ray are activated together...establishing the Christ Presence of the Seventh Ray of Spiritual Freedom into Humanity...the ascendency of the Seventh Ray expressing through every aspect of Humanity's evolving consciousness as she passes through the Cosmic Gates of Opportunity throughout this year. Hierarchs: The Great Divine Director Lord Saithrhu and our Beloved Ascended Master Saint Germain. Flame: A Cosmic Violet Flame with a planetary enfolding Golden Radiance of the Christ Presence innate within Spiritual Freedom.

E. HUMANITY'S CHRIST FLAME
AT SHAMBALLA

F. GLOBAL GROUP AVATAR'S
THREE-FOLD FLAME

G. HUMANITY'S INDIVIDUAL
THREE-FOLD FLAME

H. PHYSICAL REALITY–THE
THREE-FOLD FLAME OF
MOTHER EARTH

VIII.
EIGHTH SOLAR ASPECT OF DEITY

A. COLOR–AQUAMARINE

DIVINE QUALITIES: Clarity, Vivification, Divine Perception, Discernment, Lucidity, the Qualities of a Spiritually Free Being, Dignity, Courtesy, Royal Charm.

DIVINE INTENT: Balanced wisdom, sophic creativity, genius, inspirational, perception and intuition through balance and enlightenment, discrimination, Feminine Ray Wisdom, Buddhic, mercy, transcendant understanding, equanimity, tranquility, serenity, detachment or detached understanding, confidence in one's knowing and being Christ Conscious.

B. SUN CYCLE AND CORRESPONDING CONSTELLATION
December 22 through January 20
CAPRICORN

C. SOLAR ARCHANGEL AND ARCHAII FOR THE *EIGHTH* SOLAR ASPECT OF DEITY
Archangel Aquariel
Archaii Clarity

D. FOURTH DIMENSIONAL RETREAT OF THE SPIRITUAL HIERARCHY
The Royal Teton Focus, in which the "open door" of opportunity fully anchors the potential for planetary Christ Consciousness as the Earth makes her great leap forward in energy, vibration and consciousness into the Twelve-fold Spiral of Solar Development. Patriarch: Lord Lanto. Hierarch: Beloved Dwjal Khul, assisted by the World Teacher and many Cosmic/Ascended Beings representing the Ray of Illumined Love. Flame: Precipitation and

Reverence for all Life...Chinese Green with a Gold Radiance.

E. HUMANITY'S CHRIST FLAME AT SHAMBALLA

F. GLOBAL GROUP AVATAR'S THREE-FOLD FLAME

G. HUMANITY'S INDIVIDUAL THREE-FOLD FLAME

H. PHYSICAL REALITY–THE THREE-FOLD FLAME OF MOTHER EARTH

IX.
NINTH SOLAR ASPECT OF DEITY

A. COLOR–MAGENTA

DIVINE QUALITIES: Harmony, Balance, Solidity, Assurance; Confidence in being in the world, but not of it. Focus of the Earth Element– physical substance of the Sacred Substance of the Body Nature of Humanity.

DIVINE INTENT: Solar Fire desire, Fire of the Soul, Holy Spirit, Solar Love, the Spirit Vitality of the Universal "I AM" in eternal creation; passionate, fervent, enthusiasm, desire, electrify, exhilarate, animate. Sacred Fire Breath; to give life through baptism by Sacred Fire...restore, resurrect, arisen, vivify, catalytic, Divine Inspiration.

B. SUN CYCLE AND CORRESPONDING CONSTELLATION November 22 through December 21 SAGITTARIUS

C. SOLAR ARCHANGEL AND
ARCHAII FOR THE *NINTH*
SOLAR ASPECT OF DEITY
Archangel Anthriel
Archaii Harmony

D. FOURTH DIMENSIONAL RE-
TREAT OF THE SPIRITUAL
HIERARCHY
Shamballa, the Home of the Lord
of the World, the Home of the Flame of Humanity's
Christhood and the central authority of spiritual
evolution on this Planet. Hierarch: Our Beloved Lord
of the World, Gautama. Flame: The Three-fold Flame
of Planetary Balance.

E. HUMANITY'S CHRIST FLAME
AT SHAMBALLA

F. GLOBAL GROUP AVATAR'S
THREE-FOLD FLAME

G. HUMANITY'S INDIVIDUAL
THREE-FOLD FLAME

H. PHYSICAL REALITY–THE
THREE-FOLD FLAME OF
MOTHER EARTH

X.
TENTH SOLAR ASPECT OF DEITY

A. COLOR–GOLD

DIVINE QUALITIES: Eternal
Peace, the Great Silence, Inner Calm, Comfort, Bal-
ance, Opulence, Abundance, Prosperity, the God
Supply of all good things, Financial Freedom.

DIVINE INTENT: Integrity of one's Being, expressing God, the "I AM" Presence, on all the realms of one's existence. The Divine Victory of Christ accomplishment in the physical realm; becoming Solar Conscious; to conclude, finish, resolve the Divine Plan, to profuse the atomic realm with God's limitless Light, to complete, culminate, fulfillment. Triumphant attainment, mastery, quintessence, ascension, one's Divine Purpose fulfilled. Heaven on Earth.

B. SUN CYCLE AND CORRESPONDING CONSTELLATION
October 23 through November 21
SCORPIO

C. SOLAR ARCHANGEL AND ARCHAII FOR THE *TENTH* SOLAR ASPECT OF DEITY
Archangel Valeoel
Archaii Peace

D. FOURTH DIMENSIONAL RETREAT OF THE SPIRITUAL HIERARCHY

Temple of Peace...a personal peace, as the Christ Presence is fully established in each Lightworker...and a global peace within Humanity, knowing her planetary Christ Presence has now arisen, come again to reclaim this Earth in Love Divine. Hierarch: The Elohim of Peace, in conjunction with Lady AEoel and the Angels of the Christ Presence, one of which shall be established in the aura of every one of Humanity...sealing this Year of Opportunity in a tangible Mantle of Peace. Flame: The Three-fold Flame of Peace with a Golden Pink Radiance.

E. HUMANITY'S CHRIST FLAME AT SHAMBALLA

F. GLOBAL GROUP AVATAR'S THREE-FOLD FLAME

G. HUMANITY'S INDIVIDUAL THREE-FOLD FLAME

H. PHYSICAL REALITY–THE THREE-FOLD FLAME OF MOTHER EARTH

XI.
ELEVENTH SOLAR ASPECT OF DEITY

A. COLOR–PEACH

DIVINE QUALITIES: Divine Purpose, Fulfillment, Selfless Service, Loving life free, Happiness, Joy, Enthusiasm, Victory, the Cosmic Moment of Victorious Accomplishment.

DIVINE INTENT: Liberty and Spiritual Freedom, Electronic Light in the atomic realm and the exquisite freedom this experience brings. Being fully spiritually responsible for every particle of Light within one's Being... unconstrained by karma or ignorance... emancipation, unimpeded flow of Light, doing God's Will perfectly. Ecstacy, rapture, fully redeemed, born again into the Light, fully consecrated in Solar Consciousness, the Holiness of God in the physical realm, union with the infinite "I AM" Presence.

B. SUN CYCLE AND CORRESPONDING CONSTELLATION September 23 through October 22 LIBRA

C. SOLAR ARCHANGEL AND
ARCHAII FOR THE *ELEVENTH*
SOLAR ASPECT OF DEITY
Archangel Perpetiel
Archaii Joy

D. FOURTH DIMENSIONAL RE-
TREAT OF THE SPIRITUAL
HIERARCHY

The major focus of God Illumina-
tion for the Planet, the Meru Gods at Lake Titicaca...
the descent of the Sacred Energies of God Illumination establishing the New World of the "I AM"
Race...the planetary Christ Presence evolving
within Humanity, bringing freedom and liberty to
all. Hierarchs: God and Goddess Meru accompanied
by the love nature of Lady Nada and the Freedom
Flame of the Goddess of Liberty. Flame: Gold with a
Pink Radiance.

E. HUMANITY'S CHRIST FLAME
AT SHAMBALLA

F. GLOBAL GROUP AVATAR'S
THREE-FOLD FLAME

G. HUMANITY'S INDIVIDUAL
THREE-FOLD FLAME

H. PHYSICAL REALITY–THE
THREE-FOLD FLAME OF
MOTHER EARTH

XII.
TWELFTH SOLAR ASPECT OF DEITY

A. COLOR–OPAL

DIVINE QUALITIES: Transforma-
tion, Transfiguration, Rebirth, Rejuvenation, the
Sacred Substance of the Spirit of Humanity–focus on
the Fire Element.

DIVINE INTENT: God Being in the
body, solidity, assurance, confidence in being God in
action everywhere present on all realms. God and
flesh made one, the Christ, spiritual resoluteness,
ONE-POINTED FOCUS OF THE DOMINION OF
GOD in all realms, all spheres, all levels of consciousness...integrity, indivisibility, confidence in the
wholeness of the Divine Plan and the First Cause of
Perfection for all things. The solidity and assurance
of one's complete unity with the Universal Divine
Plan and the Cosmic "I AM" Presence.

B. SUN CYCLE AND CORRES-
PONDING CONSTELLATION
August 23 through September 22
VIRGO

C. SOLAR ARCHANGEL AND
ARCHAII FOR THE *TWELFTH*
SOLAR ASPECT OF DEITY
Archangel Omniel
Archaii Opalessence

D. FOURTH DIMENSIONAL RE-
TREAT OF THE SPIRITUAL
HIERARCHY
A Focus of Healing...the Healing
Power of the planetary Christ Presence...Humanity
developing the God Power to heal and illumine her-
self, raising all into Spiritual Freedom. Hierarchies:
the Twelve Solar Archangels, who now desire to
more closely personalize Their association with the

planetary Lightworkers to accelerate Humanity's Solar Transformation. Flame: Twelve-fold Solar Spectrum representing the Twelve-fold Aspect of Deity from the Great Central Sun.

E. HUMANITY'S CHRIST FLAME AT SHAMBALLA

F. GLOBAL GROUP AVATAR'S THREE-FOLD FLAME

G. HUMANITY'S INDIVIDUAL THREE-FOLD FLAME

H. PHYSICAL REALITY–THE THREE-FOLD FLAME OF MOTHER EARTH

NOTE: On the Angelic Harvest, September 30, 1987, the five mighty Archangels who represent the Eighth through the Twelfth Rays from the Electronic Belt around the Great Central Sun were called before the Throne of Beloved Alpha and Omega. A Divine Ceremony took place in which each Archangel and Archaii was given a staff of Power and Authority to enter the atmosphere of Earth and magnetize the additional Five Rays of Deity from the Great Central Sun into the awakening centers of Humanity. With the activities of recent years, Humanity is rising out of the frequency of a seven-fold third dimensional planetary being into the frequency of a Twelve-fold Fourth Dimensional Solar Being.

On October 6, 1987, during the full moon Lunar Eclipse, the five Archangels and Their Divine Complements, the Archaii, descended into the atmosphere of Earth, drawing with Them the five additional Rays of Deity.

These qualities of God are now available as never before to assist this sweet Earth into the Permanent Golden Age.

The Twelve Archangels and the Twelve Archaii will remain with Planet Earth until all life evolving hereon is wholly Ascended and Free.

AMPLIFYING THE TWELVE SOLAR RAYS ON EARTH
THROUGH THE GIFT OF THE DIVINE MOTHER

Beloved Mother Mary, who represents the Divine Mother Principle on Earth, has given us a sacred gift to enhance our ability to Ascend into Solar Being, the Realm of Limitless Physical Perfection.

At the inception of the last Age, the Christian Dispensation, Beloved Mother Mary volunteered to come to Earth in a physical body to offer Her vehicle as the open door through which the Avatar of that Age, Beloved Jesus, would embody in human form.

She had been trained at inner levels for centuries of time on the principles of holding the Immaculate Concept, which is the Divine Blueprint for all manifest form. As She entered the physical plane, She was entrusted with the Immaculate Concept of the Divine Plan for Beloved Jesus. Every detail of His sacred mission on Earth was recorded in Mother Mary's Heart Flame, and with every breath She took during Her Earthly sojourn, She nourished and protected that plan. With the clear vision of His Divine Plan held before Him through the concentrated efforts of Mother Mary, Beloved Jesus' mission was brought to fruition with Victorious Accomplishment. Even in the face of the most terrifying adversity, Beloved Jesus passed through His Earthly initiations into Christhood Victoriously.

As Mother Mary walked down from the hill at Golgotha after the crucifixion of Her Beloved Son, She said, "what I have done for you, my Beloved Son, I now do for all mankind." At that moment, Mother Mary's Divine service was expanded from holding the Immaculate Concept for one Avatar-Christed Being to holding the Immaculate Concept for every man, woman and child evolving on Earth until each one likewise attains the Christed state of Being and again reclaims his/her natural birthright as a Son or Daughter of God, thus Healing, once and for all, our self-inflicted separation from God.

At the inception of this New Age, the Permanent Golden Age of Spiritual Freedom, Beloved Mother Mary is again making Her presence known. She is cradling this Sweet Earth in Her Heart Flame and has asked that each of us enhance Her ability to assist the Earth and all life evolving here by balancing Her efforts. Cosmic Law states that the call for assistance must come from the realm where the assistance is needed and that the energy pouring forth from the Heavenly Realms must be balanced by Humanity's energy.

Mother Mary's symbol has always been a white rose of purity. In the past Age, She revealed to the consciousness of Humanity a prayer that would assist in balancing Her efforts to help the evolutions of Earth. This prayer was called "The Rosary."

Now, during this Cosmic Moment of planetary transformation when Mother Mary's service to Earth has been expanded to holding the Immaculate Concept for every particle of life, She again reveals to us a prayer that will increase in power a thousand times a thousand-fold each time it is recited. This invocation of unprecedented power will allow the Immaculate Concept for Planet Earth, the Divine Blueprint being held within the Mind of God, to quickly manifest. She has assured us that, as we recite this sacred prayer, our individual lives will begin to reflect clearly our Divine Purpose and reason for being. The illusion of the third dimensional plane that has trapped us in lack and limitation will be dissipated, and the reality of our Divine Heritage–Heaven on Earth–will be revealed.

Each of us must go within to the Presence of God pulsating in our hearts and evaluate, according to our wisdom and our understanding, the opportunity at hand. Then, in deep humility and gratitude, we shall recite this sacred prayer according to our inner direction.

The Rosary of the New Age

*Hail Mother, full of Grace, the Lord is with Thee.

Blessed art Thou amongst women, and Blessed is the fruit of Thy womb "I AM".

Hold for us NOW the Immaculate Concept of our true God reality from this moment unto our Eternal Ascension in the Light.

"I AM" that "I AM"

(repeat from * twelve times)

The preceding is repeated twelve times, once for each of the Rays of the twelve Solar Aspects of Deity. As each "Hail Mother..." is stated, visualize the color and qualities of the corresponding Ray entering your heart and flooding through you to bathe the Planet (see chart page 181).

After reciting the "Hail Mother..." twelve times, focusing on a different Solar Aspect each time, repeat the following command three times:

"I AM" the Immaculate Concept of my true God reality, NOW made manifest and sustained by Holy Grace. (3X)

At the conclusion of the entire series, the energy is sealed and permanently sustained by decreeing:

It is done! So be it! "I AM"!

THE ROSARY OF THE NEW AGE

Recite "Hail Mother"	Solar Aspect	Solar Archangels	Solar Archaii	Color	Qualities
1st Time	1st Ray	Michael	Faith	Blue	God's Will
2nd Time	2nd Ray	Jophiel	Constance	Yellow	Enlightenment
3rd Time	3rd Ray	Chamuel	Charity	Pink	Divine Love
4th Time	4th Ray	Gabriel	Hope	White	Purity
5th Time	5th Ray	Raphael	Mother Mary	Green	Truth
6th Time	6th Ray	Uriel	Donna Grace	Ruby	Ministering Grace
7th Time	7th Ray	Zadkiel	Holy Amethyst	Violet	Freedom
8th Time	8th Ray	Aquariel	Clarity	Aquamarine	Clarity
9th Time	9th Ray	Anthriel	Harmony	Magenta	Harmony
10th Time	10th Ray	Valeoel	Peace	Gold	Eternal Peace
11th Time	11th Ray	Perpetiel	Joy	Peach	Divine Purpose
12th Time	12th Ray	Omniel	Opalessence	Opal	Transformation

CHAPTER
FOUR

THE GIFT TO RECLAIM YOUR PROSPERITY

ELIMINATING POVERTY CONSCIOUSNESS

This is a very unique time on Planet Earth, often a confusing and frightening time. Through the advancement of modern technology, we have instant global communication, and we are constantly being informed of the extreme imbalances appearing on the screen of life. We see lack and limitation manifesting everywhere. We see hunger, homelessness and all manner of poverty. We hear dire reports of economic failure, such as the demise of the savings and loan companies or the crash of the stock market. The terms foreclosure, bankruptcy and recession are becoming household words. Companies are going out of business daily, and the jobless rate is increasing. There is a prevailing sense of uncertainty and fear that runs through all economic circles and the general public as well. This sense of fear is creating a consciousness of panic that is casting caution to the wind. The insidious influence of greed and selfishness is tightening its paralyzing grip. When this occurs, integrity and social conscience are swept aside. The environment is ignored, and the well-being of Humanity and the Earth itself are jeopardized in pursuit of the almighty dollar.

Even though this is a very difficult time on Earth, a period that was biblically referred to as "the time of the screaming and the gnashing of the teeth," the purging that is taking place throughout the economic world is a necessary, critical part of the planetary transformation that is now at hand.

For aeons of time the monitary system of the world has been abused. Instead of the natural exchange of give and take, based on the principle of always working toward the highest good for all concerned, the wealth of the world has been used by the elite few to manipulate, dominate, oppress and control the multitudes.

Money has been such a source of pain and suffering throughout history that religious orders in both Eastern and Western cultures considered money itself to be innately evil. They, thereby, denounced it and actually took vows of poverty. This action gave the spiritual aspirants of the world the message that somehow poverty was a virtue. Interestingly, this belief system perpetuated the schism between the haves and the have nots. It also created a phenomenon that intensified the abuse of money because the people who were truly seeking greater levels of truth to improve the quality of life on the Planet and those who genuinely were striving toward spiritual growth and self-mastery were being taught by the world religions that money was evil and should not be acquired. That belief left the money in the hands of those who were not pursuing the highest good for all, but rather pursuing the self-indulgent gratification of greed and power. Because the abuse of money has been the order of the day on Earth for literally millenniums, we probably all have etheric records and memories of times when we either abused our wealth or when others used their wealth to abuse us. These etheric records vibrate at a subconscious level, but they can be very effective at repelling money away from us. In either case, whether we were the abused or the abuser, or on occasion both, the message was that money is a source of pain. It is very hard to get past that subconscious block and allow money into our lives when we keep associating money with pain.

This is truly a cosmic moment on Earth, a moment being referred to as the dawn of the Permanent Golden Age. In this dawning age, it has been decreed by Divine Fiat that Heaven shall manifest on Earth. As you can well imagine, poverty, homelessness, lack and limitation do not exist in Heaven. Consequently, that means that they will not exist on Earth either when the transformation is complete. But, what we must realize is that they are not going to be eliminated because someone waves a wand and magically makes them disappear. They are going to be eliminated because you and I and every other person evolving on Earth learns to apply the Laws of Prosperity accurately and effectively in our lives.

At any given moment our environment is reflecting a sum total of our thoughts, words, actions, feelings and beliefs. The world at large is a reflection of Humanity's consciousness. What is occurring now, in the global economy, is not

God punishing us for our past abuse of money as some are indicating, but instead, it is our own energy returning to us to allow us to experience the results of our actions. At this critical time of change, if there is any area in our lives where we are not reaching our highest potential, it is being pushed to the surface in such a way that we don't have any choice but to face it and deal with it. We are no longer being allowed by our Higher Selves to stuff or deny problem areas. Needless to say, poverty is a problem area, and it is surfacing in people's lives throughout the world in a very painful way. Even though we don't like pain, we seem to use it as our motivator. As long as we are comfortable, we will be willing to stagnate forever, but if we experience a real crisis in our lives, we begin to scramble around to try and alleviate it. That is what is happening now in the world of the economy. We have strayed far from the original Divine Plan as far as money goes, and we must now clear up our past mistakes and get back on track.

The imbalance and failure of our economic system that is now being brought to our awareness through the media is surfacing so that we can clearly see the error of our ways of greed and selfishness, so that, through greater insight and understanding, we will create an economic system that reflects a reverence for ALL life and the highest good for all concerned.

Abundance is actually our natural state of being. The supply of the Universe is limitless. When the Earth was created, God provided Humanity with everything we needed to abide in this verdant paradise of splendor, including the knowledge and wisdom to sustain a life of prosperity and abundance. It was only when we began to use our gift of free will to express thoughts and feelings that reflected a consciousness of less than prosperity that we began to experience lack and limitation.

We must remember that our thoughts are creative. Whatever we put our attention and energy into, whatever we think and feel, we bring into form. When Humanity began to express thoughts and feelings of fear and poverty, these discordant vibrations began to reflect on the atomic substance of physical matter in this third dimensional plane. Then, instead of the continual manifestation of the God supply of all good things, we began to experience extreme imbalances and impoverishment. The Elemental Kingdom, which always reflects Humanity's consciousness, began to show signs of decay and degeneration. Floods, famines, draughts and pestilence became the order of the day. The people evolving on Earth observed the changes taking place, and they became more fearful and confused. This negative state of consciousness perpetuated even greater degrees of lack and scarcity. Thus, over aeons of time, Humanity created a building momentum of poverty consciousness. We became deeply entrenched in the discordant thoughtforms of limitation. We observed the indigence of the outer world and accepted it as our natural state of being. We forgot that we were co-creators in our Earthly experience. We lost the awareness that the things occurring in our lives were merely a reflection of our thoughts, words, feelings, actions and beliefs. Instead, we looked at the poverty of the world and tried to justify it by proclaiming it to be God's Will. We felt victimized and tried to outsmart our so-called lot in life. We became conniving and deceitful. We believed that the only way we could have *enough,* was to take things away from others. This attitude became the basis for all of our wars, greed and selfishness. The momentum of poverty consciousness increased throughout the ages of time, and, day by day, we methodically sank into our present level of degradation.

If we will objectively observe the negative things occurring in the world, we will see that almost every single destructive expression of life is, in some way, reflecting a belief in lack and limitation and also reflecting the actions of greed and selfishness that naturally accompany that belief system. This material spiral into oblivion must now come to an end. It is critical, for the survival of the Planet, that we turn away from the distorted acceptance of poverty and begin clearly and effectively developing a consciousness of prosperity. Poverty is in absolute opposition to the Divine Plan for the Earth and all of Humanity evolving upon her. Poverty cannot exist in the presence of Light, and the Earth is destined to be a Planet of Light.

There are millions of souls now evolving on Earth who are awakening to the inner knowledge that recorded deep within their cellular memories is the understanding of the Laws of Prosperity. These souls know, through every fiber of their beings, that God is their supply, and they know that supply is limitless. Yet, their life experience is still reflecting signs of the lack of financial sustenance. This paradox confirms the fact that even the illumined souls on Earth who have the intellectual knowledge and wisdom of the Laws of Prosperity, have powerful etheric records and memories based in poverty consciousness that repel money away from them.

In order for us to eliminate the manifestation of poverty in our lives we must fully participate in a two-fold activity of Light. First, we must release and transmute all of the etheric records and memories of the past that vibrate at any level of poverty consciousness. Second, we must create a new etheric blueprint of prosperity consciousness and reprogram that blueprint into every level of our minds, feelings, actions and beliefs.

Because of the urgency of the hour and the criticalness of this moment on Earth, God and the Legions of Light Who abide in the Heavenly Realms to do His Will, have evaluated Humanity's greatest need. It has been determined that even the illumined souls, the Lightworkers, have too far to go to truly eliminate poverty in their lives through the natural progression of evolution in time to turn things around before it is too late. Consequently, it has been decreed by Cosmic Law that Divine Intervention is necessary.

The Light on the Planet has been increasing daily and hourly for several years. Through the unified efforts of millions of Lightworkers who have joined together in consciousness for global meditations of World Peace and Planetary Healing, a Planetary security system of Divine Love has formed around the Earth. This security system, which expands from heart center to heart center among the Lightworkers, is also anchored deep into the crystal grid system of the physical substance of Earth. The vibratory rate of the

Planet is increasing. Whenever large numbers of souls volunteer to selflessly expand the Light of the world, special cosmic dispensations are granted and additional amounts of Light from the Heart of God are released to balance Humanity's efforts. The additional allotment of energy is always released into the world in a way that will fulfill Humanity's greatest need. It has been determined by the Godhead that Humanity's greatest need of the hour is THE ELIMINATION OF POVERTY AND THE ACTIVATION OF THE FLOW OF ABUNDANCE INTO THE LIVES OF THE LIGHTWORKERS ON EARTH.

As mentioned earlier, the illumined souls who are truly striving to improve the quality of life on the Planet and who are determined that the highest good for ALL concerned shall manifest with a reverence for ALL life, often consider poverty to be a virtue. This is creating a very difficult challenge. With the increased influx of Light, the illumined souls are awakening. They are learning to reach into the Divine Mind of God and tap the wisdom and knowledge of the Ages that will reveal viable solutions to the world's woes. But, they do not have the financial sustenance to bring these glorious ideas into physical reality.

As we awaken, we begin to perceive the magnitude of our purpose and reason for being. As the Divine Ideas from the Mind of God flow into our consciousness, we are recognizing ways and means of developing tangible alternatives to our present course of action which appears to be planetary destruction. The ideas are wonderful and resonate with mutual respect for all life on Planet Earth. There are ideas for alternative energy and fuel systems that will not pollute the air or use up our limited resources; ideas for alternative plans for food production that will feed the entire Planet; ideas for alternative economic systems that will bring prosperity and abundance to all Humanity; ideas for alternative health systems that will allow each person access to the optimum treatment for their particular affliction; ideas for alternative ways of disposing of and recycling our excess so that our Beloved Earth will flourish, and there are limitless other ideas for alternatives that will transform this Planet into Freedom's

Holy Star.

It is time for us to recognize and accept that we live in the physical plane of existence, and we must deal with the physical reality. This means that if we are going to bring the new innovative ideas into physical manifestation, we must utilize the existing means of exchange, which at the present time, is a monetary system. It is time for the Lightworkers of the world to open up to the limitless flow of God's abundance, so we can have the necessary monetary exchange to accomplish the magnificent goals and ideas pouring into our consciousness from the Realms of Illumined Truth. It is time to bring these ideas into physical reality.

In order to help us accomplish this, we are being given superhuman assistance. The entire Company of Heaven is joining forces in this endeavor, and the opportunity being presented to us to achieve PERMANENT FINANCIAL FREEDOM is unprecedented. But, we must remember not even God will interfere with our gift of free will. In order for us to fully benefit from this unparalleled opportunity, we must take the necessary action and choose, on a conscious level, to release and transmute all past acceptance of poverty –cause, core, effect, record and memory. We must also transmute, through the power of forgiveness, all we have ever done to abuse the substance of money, all we have ever done to manipulate, dominate, control or hurt any part of life through selfishness, greed or the misuse of money. We must also forgive all those who, in any way, used the substance of money to abuse us. We must literally go back in consciousness, through the ages of time, and ask God to transmute every electron of precious life energy we have ever misqualified in relation to money. This must penetrate into every existence and dimension we have ever experienced, both known and unknown, piercing deep into every electron we have ever released that is vibrating at a frequency less than absolute abundance, prosperity, opulence, the God supply of all good things and financial freedom.

In order for us to accomplish this incredible feat in the time allotted, we are receiving Divine intervention. The most intensified activity of the Law of Forgiveness ever manifest in the history of time is being released into the atmosphere of Earth. This Violet Light is pouring forth from the very Heart of God, and It is vibrating at frequencies of the Fifth Dimension. These are frequencies of perfection that we have never before been able to withstand on Earth.

Since the shift of vibration that took place on the Planet during Harmonic Convergence (August 15, 16 & 17, 1987) the vibratory rate of Earth has been increasing daily and hourly the maximum that we can withstand. We are now capable of withstanding more Light than ever before. It is crucial that we clearly understand, even though this glorious Light of forgiveness is available for us to use to transmute our past actions and beliefs which are anchored in poverty consciousness, the only way we will experience the effect of this gift tangibly in our everyday lives is to draw it through our Heart Flame and consciously project it into the physical plane. It has always been said "God needs a body." The Law is that in order for something to manifest in the physical plane, it must be drawn through the Divine Spark pulsating in the heart of someone abiding in the physical plane. This simply means that, even though this splendid gift is pouring into the atmosphere of Earth, if we don't invoke it into our lives and project it into our life experience through our thoughts, words, actions and feelings, we will not receive its benefits or create a life of permanent financial freedom for ourselves.

Fortunately, the entire Company of Heaven Who always function under the auspices of Divine Order, never release such a gift to the finite minds of Humanity without releasing the wisdom and understanding of how to effectively utilize such a precious gift. We have been given a guided visualization and an activity of Light by the Realms of Illumined Truth that will enable each and every one of us to take advantage of this momentous opportunity.

Utilizing the Violet Light of Forgiveness completes the first step of the two-fold activity of Light that is necessary to eliminate poverty in our lives. Now, we must take the second step which involves creating a new etheric blueprint of prosperity consciousness and integrating that Divine pattern into every level of our minds, feelings, actions and beliefs.

The time is so very short before the Earth must reclaim her Divine heritage and again manifest Heaven on Earth as decreed through the Lord's Prayer, "Thy Kingdom come, Thy Will be done on Earth as it is in Heaven." A clarion call is reverberating throughout the Universe invoking assistance for Planet Earth. The response is coming from myriad Legions of Illumined Beings. These glorious Beings of Light are descending into the atmosphere of Earth. They are magnetizing the Eternal Light of God that is always Victorious into the Earth. As one unified Presence, one Holy Breath, one heartbeat, one thought, one energy and vibration, one consciousness of pure God Light, these Divine Beings are creating a cosmic forcefield in the atmosphere of Earth that has the capability of transforming the distorted experience of poverty back into the original Divine Plan which is the continual flow of God's abundance into the everyday lives of all lifestreams evolving on Earth. This forcefield has the power to change our Earthly experience at an atomic cellular level and will shift our vibratory rate into the new etheric blueprint of prosperity. This sacred gift is available to all who choose to lift up in consciousness and magnetize its Holy Essence into the physical plane of Earth. We have been given a guided visualization that will assist each of us to do just that.

The wonderful thing about the Divine Intervention taking place on Earth is that we don't have to fully understand it. We don't have to believe it; we don't even have to accept it. All we have to do to benefit from it is ask, through the Presence of God anchored in our hearts, that it flow into our lives. The Law is "ask and you shall receive; knock and the door will be open." If you will trust enough to ask God to allow these Divine gifts to flow into your life, on the return current of that very plea, you will begin to experience the frequencies of prosperity.

Read this chapter, or listen to the tape associated with this chapter, over and over again. Ask the Presence of God pulsating within you to filter out every trace of human consciousness and accept only the words that resonate as truth in your own heart. Do the exercises and visualizations daily, and know that, each time this chapter is read, or the tape is played, it adds to the building momentum of prosperity consciousness in your own individual life and in the lives of all Humanity as well. Step by step your physical reality will begin to change, and instead of reflecting lack and limitation, your life will reflect the God supply of all good things: prosperity, abundance, opulence and financial freedom.

CLAIMING YOUR PROSPERITY

The Divine gifts from the Realms of Perfection that are being made available to all Humanity during this Cosmic Moment of planetary transformation must be magnetized into the physical plane of Earth through our true God reality, our Higher Self and not through our lower human ego.

Our lower human ego is composed of a synthesis of all the activities we have expressed through our physical, etheric, mental and emotional bodies during our Earthly sojourn. This part of our identity was created gradually as we experienced life through our limited physical senses. Much of the poverty Humanity has experienced is because we have perceived the lower human ego to be an intelligence apart from God. We have given it power and dominion by accepting and believing that this limited, struggling self is who we really are. We lost the awareness of our true God Self, and as a result, we have bound ourselves in the distorted perception of extreme lack and limitation. As long as we believe we are separate from God, we will experience the painful conditions of poverty. Only when we accept our true God reality will we allow God's limitless abundance to flow into our lives. When we actually accept our God Presence *as* ourselves and not some separate "self" we occasionally call upon, our lives will reflect an entirely new picture, and instead of poverty, we will create prosperity. We are now being given the opportunity, through Divine Intervention, to pass over the threshold into individual and planetary transformation.

Our God Self is One with the all-encompassing Presence of God, and It continually prods and prompts us ever onward to our highest potential. When we give our God Self dominion in our lives, we are lifted into octaves of awareness and understanding that enable us to clearly KNOW "all that the Father has is mine." We recognize that prosperity is our natural state of being, and abundance is available in every aspect of our lives now.

As we harmoniously focus our attention on the perfection of our true God Self, our lower human personality is lifted up and integrated into that radiant Presence of Light. Then we are able to function on Earth as the children of God we truly are.

We accomplish this integration by going within and re-establishing a loving relationship with our God Self. When we do this, we begin to recognize and accept our God Self. An awakening takes place, and we begin to activate within our consciousness the deep memory that has always known of our Divinity. From this level of consciousness, we know through every fiber of our beings, "I AM" unlimited prosperity; "I AM" the continual flow of God's abundance. We understand that this Presence of God always pulsates within our hearts, and It is all knowing, all caring, all loving and all powerful.

When we reunite with our God Presence, Divine energy flows in and through us. This Divine energy is the fulfillment of every good and perfect thing. It is completely impersonal, and when it flows through our newly developed forcefield of God consciousness, it has no choice but to manifest perfection here and now. Prosperity is then reclaimed as our natural state of being.

Now, it is time for each of us to utilize the full power of our Divinity, our God Self, to invoke into our lives the full gathered momentum of the sacred gift of the Violet Light of Forgiveness; the gift which is pouring forth into the atmosphere of Earth from the very Heart of God; the gift which is being given to Humanity at this Cosmic Moment to transmute all frequencies of poverty consciousness; the gift which represents the greatest influx of the Law of Forgiveness ever manifest in the history of time.

After we invoke the Violet Light of Forgiveness together as one unified consciousness, we will join with the entire Company of Heaven and magnetize the cosmic forcefield of prosperity that is pulsating in the atmosphere into the everyday lives of all Lightworkers evolving on Planet Earth.

All is in readiness. To participate in this Divine activity of Light, please sit comfortably in your chair with your arms and legs uncrossed, your spine as straight as possible and your hands resting gently in your lap with your palms facing upward.

Breathe in deeply, and as you exhale, let all of the tension of the day just drop away, and feel yourself becoming completely relaxed. Breathe in deeply again, and as you exhale, feel your God Self take full dominion of your four lower bodies. Your mind is activated. The cobwebs of confusion or doubt or fear are swept away, and you become mentally alert and vibrantly aware. You realize that, through the radiance of your God Presence, you are enveloped in a forcefield of invincible protection which prevents anything that is not of the Light from distracting you or interfering with this sacred moment.

You feel the deep inner glow of peace and well-being. You experience the buoyant joy of expectancy and enthusiasm. You accept that you are the open door that no one can shut.

Now, I would like for you to follow me through this visualization with the full power of your attention. I will write in the first person so each of us can experience this activity of Light tangibly and personally in our own life.

Beloved Presence of God blazing in my heart...I know and accept that, through this invocation, you have taken command of my four lower bodies. My physical, etheric, mental and emotional bodies are now being raised up in vibration, and they are being integrated with your radiant Presence. My awareness is increasing, and I begin to perceive clearly Your "still, small voice within." I know that you respond to my every call for assistance. I am beginning to experience your exquisite vibrations, and my entire being is flooded with Light. My consciousness is opening to the influx of your pure spiritual energy. From this new level of awareness, I now know, as never before, You are in me, and "I Am" in Thee. I KNOW You are me.

"I Am" a Being of Radiant Light! "I Am" one with the energy and vibration that is the all encompassing Presence of God.

"I Am" one with the Divine Love that fills the Universe with the glory of Itself.

"I Am" one with every particle of life. "I Am" one with the Divine Plan for Planet Earth.

"I Am" one with the limitless flow of God's abundance.

"I Am" that "I Am".

A reactivation and initiation into multi-dimensional awareness is occurring within me.

"I Am" being lifted up, closer in vibration to the very Heart of God. The pre-encoded memories that were implanted deep within my cellular patterns aeons ago are being activated. These patterns reveal my Divine Plan, my purpose and reason for being. "I Am" experiencing a great soaring and awakening as I begin to remember my Divine Heritage.

"I Am" stepping through the doorway into multi-dimensional reality. Here "I Am" being empowered with even more rarified frequencies of Divinity. Moment to moment, this radiant Light is awakening within me previously untapped levels of wisdom and illumination. I easily grasp each Divine thought and idea. As I do, avenues of opportunity begin to unfold before me. I feel a sense of elation as each opportunity presents itself. I joyously seize the Divine opportunities, and I feel a greater sense of self-worth and accomplishment than ever before. My Life is pulsating with a sense of meaning and warmth. "I AM" now being lifted higher into the Realms of Perfection…and now higher… and now higher.

In this realm, I easily release and let go of attachments and behavior patterns that do not support my highest good. I release all patterns that reflect a consciousness less than prosperity. I recognize *this is the moment of my new beginning*.

I now have the absolute ability to change and create prosperity consciousness, and I move into change easily and joyously.

"I Am" experiencing my true integrity. "I Am" trustworthy and honest. "I Am" an expression of Divine Truth.

"I Am" worthy and deserving of prosperity, and "I Am" able to transform every aspect of my life now.

Change is manifesting through Divine Grace and Love. As each aspect of my life that needs changing surfaces before me, I easily love it free and forgive myself for my perceived transgression.

I know "I Am" a child of God, and I deserve to be loved and forgiven. As the changes take place, "I Am" experiencing a sense of inner calm, patience and silence.

"I Am" in the Divine flow of my true God reality. "I Am" one with the Infinite Intelligence within me, and "I Am" now able to always make correct choices. I love myself unconditionally, and "I Am" grateful for this opportunity to change, which I accept with deep humility.

The Divine Power to sustain these changes is continually flowing through me, and from this moment forth, I choose to create a life of prosperity and only that which supports my highest good.

Once again "I Am" lifted higher into the Realms of Perfection…and now higher…and now higher.

I begin to focus on the sacred essence of my Holy Breath.

I realize that with every inbreath I extend in consciousness, through my eternal journey into Infinity, to the Source of never ending perfection, and with every outbreath, I magnetize the full momentum of that perfection and radiate its full blessing to all life evolving in Earth.

My inbreath is the open portal to the pure land of boundless splendor and infinite Light, and my outbreath is the source of all Divine blessings for Humanity and the Planet. I understand now that the Divine gifts being presented to Humanity from the Legions of Light serving this sweet Earth will be drawn into the world of form on the Holy Breath.

I consecrate and dedicate myself to be the open door for these sacred gifts of Light. Lord, make me an instrument of Your limitless abundance. "I AM" the Flaming Hand of God, now made manifest in the physical plane of Earth.

"I Am" now ready, through every level of my consciousness, to release, let go of and transmute every frequency of vibration, every single electron of precious life energy I have ever released in any existence or dimension that is expressing a pattern less than God's limitless flow of abundance, prosperity, opulence, the supply of all good things and financial freedom.

"I Am" enveloped in an invincible forcefield of protection and eternal peace. From within this, "I Am" able to review my life as an objective observer. I ask my God Self to push to the surface of my conscious mind every experience I have ever had, both known and unknown, that is, in any way, preventing me from attaining prosperity. As these experiences begin to surface, I breathe in deeply, and on the Holy Breath, I pierce into the gift of the Violet Light of Forgiveness. I absorb the most powerful gift of forgiveness ever manifest in the history of time, and I breathe it in, through and around my four lower vehicles, and all of the energy surfacing and returning to me now to be loved free. This sacred Violet Light from the very Heart of God instantly transmutes the negative thoughts, words, actions, feelings, beliefs and memories that are blocking my eternal financial freedom. Every electron of energy is being transformed back into its original perfection.

My God Self now expands this activity of Light and reaches back into the ages of time to magnetize every electron of energy stamped with my individual electronic pattern into the gift of the Violet Light of Forgiveness. These records and memories surface effortlessly, and "I Am" able to let them go without pain or fear. I feel the buoyant joy of freedom.

I continue breathing in as I reach deeper into the sacred gift of Violet Light, and I exhale its Divine essence to flood the physical plane of Earth.

I affirm with deep feeling and a true inner knowing...

"I Am" a force of the Violet Light of Forgiveness
    greater than anything less than prosperity.

I now realize "I Am" able to transmute, through the power of this sacred gift, the mass consciousness of poverty. All records and memories of Humanity's abuse of the substance of money begin to flow into the Violet Light of Forgiveness.

Under the direction of my God Self and the entire Company of Heaven, every electron of poverty consciousness that has ever been released by any part of life, in any existence or dimension, both known and unknown, is surfacing for transmutation by the Violet Light of Forgiveness.

The transformation is taking place as each electron enters the Violet Light and is instantly transmuted–cause, core, effect, record and memory–back into the frequencies of prosperity and God's limitless abundance.

"I Am" a force of the Violet Light of Forgiveness,
    greater than anything less than prosperity.
"I Am" a force of the Violet Light of Forgiveness,
    greater than anything less than prosperity.
"I Am" a force of the Violet Light of Forgiveness,
    greater than anything less than prosperity.
"I Am" Free! "I Am" Free! "I Am" Free!
"I Am" Eternally Financially Free!
It is done! So be it! "I Am"!

I ask, through the Presence of God pulsating in my heart, that this sacred activity of Light be maintained, eternally self-sustained, increased with my every breath, daily and hourly, moment to moment, the maximum that Cosmic Law will allow, until all life, belonging to or serving the Earth at this time is wholly ascended and free.

"I Am" now lifted up in consciousness even higher into the Realms of Perfection...and now higher...and now higher.

I pass over the Highway of Light that bridges Heaven and Earth. I enter the pure land of boundless splendor and infinite Light that radiates in the atmosphere of Earth, and I KNOW the Father and I are One.

All the Lightworkers evolving on Earth are joining me in consciousness in this Octave of Pure Joy. I know "I Am" one with every part of life. As one unified voice, we send forth the clarion call into the Universe invoking our illumined brothers and sisters to come and help us in our moment of transformation. The Cosmic tone of our unified voice reverberates through all dimensions, and the response comes from every corner of the Cosmos.

We see the luminous Presence of Legions of Divine Beings descending into the atmosphere of Earth. They take Their strategic positions above us and begin forming a tremendous circle as They stand shoulder to shoulder.

As one unified consciousness, one Holy Breath, one heartbeat, one energy and vibration of perfection, They begin to breathe into Their Heart Flames the Golden Ray of Eternal Peace and Opulence from the very Heart of God. This resplendent Golden Light contains within Its Holy vibration every frequency of God's abundance. It is the most glorious, scintillating color gold we have ever seen. As these magnificent Beings absorb the essence of Opulence into Their Heart Flames, They become blazing Golden Suns of Light. They now, in perfect synchronicity, breathe the Golden Light into the center of the circle. As the Golden Rays of Light pour forth from Their Heart centers into the center of the circle, the Rays begin to merge, forming a brilliant Golden Sun. This Sun is the matrix within which the Cosmic force-field of Prosperity Consciousness will form.

The Beings of Light now begin magnetizing the thoughtform of the forcefield of prosperity which is being held in the Divine Mind of God. The blueprint begins forming within the Golden Sun. It is a radiant, brilliant Golden Pyramid of Light, and pulsating within Its base is a shimmering Golden Lotus Blossom. With each pulsation of the Lotus Blossom, concentric circles of Divine Opulence are projected into the physical plane of Earth to bathe every particle of life evolving here in the glory of God's abundance. Unformed primal Light substance is now being magnetized into the etheric blueprint, and the Golden Pyramid of Opulence becomes tangibly manifest. Its resplendent beauty will pulsate continually in the atmosphere of Earth, sustained through the unified efforts of the entire Company of Heaven until all life evolving here is wholly Ascended and Free.

Now, the Lightworkers of the world prepare to be the open portals through which this Divine Gift of Prosperity will manifest in the world of form.

The Flame of Divinity, blazing in every human heart, begins expanding to envelop the four lower bodies of each Lightworker. We experience a beautiful Blue Flame blazing through the left side of our bodies. This is the Masculine Polarity of God qualified with Divine Will and Power. We experience a beautiful Pink Flame blazing through the right side of our bodies. This is the Feminine Polarity of God qualified with Divine Love. As the Masculine and Feminine Polarities of God are balanced within us, we experience the expansion of the Sunshine Yellow Flame of God which is qualified with Divine Wisdom and Illumination.

We are now enveloped in the Victorious Three-fold Flame, and we are the expression of our true God Self grown to full stature.

From this consciousness of Divinity, we begin to magnetize a Golden Ray of Light from the tremendous Pyramid of Prosperity into our heart centers. As the Ray of Light merges with the Spark of Divinity in our hearts, a miniature replica of the Golden Pyramid with the Golden Lotus Blossom pulsating in its base is formed. This creates a magnetic forcefield in our hearts that enables us to draw the full momentum of blessings from this sacred Pyramid into our everyday life experience.

We breathe in deeply, and as we do, we pierce into the Golden Pyramid of Light. We absorb the Golden Light of Opulence pulsating from the Lotus Blossom, and, as we exhale, a cascading fountain of Golden Light pours through our heart centers into the physical plane of Earth. This sacred Light of God's abundance floods the Planet and flows into the hands of every Lightworker, every activity of Light, every conscious person who will, in any way, shape or form, use this Gift of Prosperity to improve the quality of life on Earth. Through this gift, the substance of money becomes tangibly available and flows continually into the hands and use of every lifestream, organization or activity that is receiving the ideas from the Divine Mind of God to restore this Planet to her Divine Heritage which is Heaven on Earth. The money flows easily and effortlessly into the tangible use of all on the Planet who are operating from a consciousness of Reverence for ALL Life.

As the Golden Light of Prosperity reaches its furthest destination in the world of form, flooding every particle of life with financial sustenance, it begins its return journey back to the Source. It flows back first to the Heart Flame that sent it forth. As this Sacred Light flows back into our hearts, it brings with It the limitless flow of money and the God Supply of all good things. Our lives now reflect the Gift of Permanent Financial Freedom. From this moment forth, every thing we need to fulfill our Divine Plans is always available to us. The Divine Law of "ask and you shall receive" is instantly manifest. We feel the buoyancy and elation of our newfound freedom, and the entire Company of Heaven rejoices with us as we reclaim our Divine Birthright of abundance through Prosperity Consciousness.

*"I Am"! "I Am"! "I Am"!

The eternally sustained manifestation of God's limitless supply of money and every good thing I require to assist me in my service to the Light, now made manifest and sustained by Holy Grace. (3X)*

It is done! So be it! "I Am"!

I now breathe in deeply and return my consciousness to the room. I become aware of my physical body and gently move my hands and feet.

"I Am" aware that "I Am" a multi-dimensional being, and I abide at once in both the pure land of boundless splendor and infinite Light and the physical world of form on Earth.

With my every breath, "I Am" continually an open portal for the full magnitude of the sacred gifts of Prosperity to pour into the everyday lives of all the Lightworkers and all activities of Light on the Planet.

I realize that each time I read the chapter, play the Prosperity tape or consciously energize this thoughtform, the sacred gifts of Prosperity will build in momentum and effectiveness. Moment by moment the transformation will occur, and the new etheric blueprint of abundance for all life, embraced within the Divine understanding of reverence, mutual respect and a consciousness of always seeking the highest good for all concerned, will become the order of the new Cosmic Day.

Tape associated with this chapter–"The Gift to Reclaim Your Prosperity."

See Page 219 for Order Form

EPILOGUE

INTERESTING NEWSPAPER ARTICLES THAT CONFIRM THE CHANGES OCCURRING IN OUR SOLAR SYSTEM

We have been advised by the Realms of Illumined Truth that the frequency of Earth is being accelerated. We are moving into the Fourth Dimension, and we are ascending into a new spiral of Evolution. We can easily observe the changes taking place on Earth and confirm that information for ourselves, but it's fun to see it confirmed through the field of science, as well. The following newspaper articles reflect the "new discoveries" of science.

BILLION WATTS OF NEW ENERGY BOMBARDING EARTH
Science Confirms What We Already Know
Quartus Report by John Randolph Price

"For years we have been talking about the new energy that is coming in from the Higher Planes—enabling Earth to rise into a higher electromagnetic field 'with a dramatic acceleration taking place in this century'... 'spiritual energy as cosmic rays has been focused on the field of Humanity's consciousness... in the form of a gentle radiation to soften hearts and open minds. As the radiation continues, a new love vibration will be the instrument to modify behavior, change attitudes, and dissolve the destructive patterns buried deeply in the collective consciousness.' (Quotes from *With Wings As Eagles*)

"We have also discussed how this new energy can cause great strain in the mental-emotion-physical system as it works to root out false beliefs and lifts us into a higher consciousness.

"Now the Associated Press, in an article on the possible causes of the ozone depletion (May 22, 1987), reports that 'electron showers have been detected by an instrument aboard a satellite. Each of the showers dumps about a billion watts of energy a second into the atmosphere, according to the Los Alamos National Laboratory. The electrons tend to spiral down the Planet's magnetic field lines. The electron showers, which hit every 27 days and last 2½ days, appear to come from Jupiter, the Sun, or both, the lab said.'

"Electrons are the electrical charges whirling around the nucleus of atoms, which cause atoms to cluster in an energy field. So an 'electron shower' would seem to indicate the appearance of new energy field being stepped down to the physical plane.

"Let's look again at the primary source as given in the report: Jupiter. And what is the significance of this Planet? In Rodney Collin's *Celestial Influence* he writes: 'The system of Jupiter seems to present an exact model of the Solar System. There are a number of implications of the highly developed state of Jupiter's system...in the first place, the influence or radiation produced by such a system must be an extremely subtle one (gentle radiation?) incorporating a large number of different frequencies in a harmonic relation. Moreover, the fact that Jupiter's system is a scale-model of the whole Solar System brings other implications. We supposed the structure of man to be an image of that of the Solar System, and the endocrine glands in him to correspond to the various planets...Jupiter by its place in the Solar System appears to emit a 'note' or frequency which activates the posterior pituitary gland and produces in it a corresponding rhythm... a feminine significance (energy) in the posterior lobe.'

"We find that the energy radiation from Jupiter is a 'healing and harmonizing' energy (words used consistently throughout Chapter One of *The Planetary Commission* and the call for the global mind-link). Collin goes on to say that the energy of Jupiter 'should be reflected in a universal fluctuation of the gentler and more Humanitarian instincts of man...in general, in the more humane aspects of human life.'

"The AP report mentioned that the energy hits Earth every 27 days. Is it just a coincidence that in numerology, 27 is nine–the ancient number symbolizing initiation? It was also called the number of man.

"And while it may be a totally unrelated phenomena, the New York Times Service reported on May 24th that 'The violent stellar explosion that flared into view over the Southern Hemisphere on February 23 has apparently spawned a mysterious twin, according to scientists at the Harvard-Smithsonian Center for Astrophysics. The observations show that the bright exploding star, or supernova, is two points of light, close together, one about 10 times brighter than its companion. Since neither was present before the explosion, astronomers assume that, mysteriously, both arose from the same blast.'

"What was released in that explosion? Yes, 'two points of light, one about 10 times brighter than its companion.' But what/who do the lights represent? Regardless of the light year-time factor, the effect in Humanity's consciousness is now.

"Perhaps the lights are the symbol of a revelation. In her book, *From Bethlehem to Calvary*, Alice Bailey writes: 'Christ Himself tells us that at the end of the age the sign of the Son of Many will be seen in the Heavens (Matt. 24:30). Just as the Birth at Bethlehem was ushered in by a Sign, that of the Star, so shall that birth toward which the race is hastening be likewise ushered in by a heavenly Sign. The appeal which goes up from the hearts of all true aspirants to initiation is beautifully embodied in the following prayer:

There is a peace that passeth understanding; it abides in the Hearts of those who live in the Eternal. There is a power which maketh all things new. It lives and moves in those who know the self as One. May that peace brood over us; that power uplift us, till we stand where the One Initiator is invoked, till we see His star shine forth.

"'When that Sign is seen and the Word is heard, the next step will be the recording of the Vision.'

"As I typed the above lines I began to feel a tingling sensation all over—and my mind instantly recalled the dream on April 5th: 'Those in spiritual light, imprinting a higher vision, will share in a new beginning.' Suddenly everything seems to come together...the Global Mind-Link on World Healing Day, December 31st...the stellar explosion on Feb-

ruary 23rd...the discovery of the twin lights which was actually made on March 24...the dream about the vision and the
soft clay on April 5th...the showers of new energy bombarding the Earth reported on May 22nd...the opportunity to im-
press the new Vision on August 16th and 17th. Is 'something' shaping up? Is a pattern emerging? Is there any reality
to all of this?

"We shall see."

PHYSICISTS THEORIZE BEAM IN SPACE HAS NEW PARTICLES

(Reprinted from The Arizona Daily Star,
October 11, 1988)

ALBUQUERQUE (AP)–A powerful beam striking the
Earth from a twin star system 14,000 light years away could
herald a new type of particle that physicists said confounds
the standard theories of physics.

The beam, carrying a million billion electron volts of
energy, comes from a neutron star, half of a binary star system named Hercules X-1 in the constellation Hercules, said
Dr. Guarang Yodh, a physicst at the University of California
at Irvine.

The neutron star is nearly the size of Earth's moon, but is
extremely dense with a mass nearly double the sun's.

The other half of the star system, about 4 million miles
from the neutron star, is a large, spinning magnet, generating massive electromagnetic fields and giving off powerful
radiation.

The beam, first detected at Los Alamos National Laboratory in July 1986, initially was believed to be electrically neutral gamma rays, which are high-energy light waves or
photons.

The problem with that interpretation was that the beam

"hits way up in the atmosphere and produces a shower of particles," Yodh said Friday in a telephone interview.

Gamma rays are not supposed to do that, said Dr. Darragh Nagle, a physicist at the Los Alamos lab.

"That's the thing that's interesting and puzzling about the finding," he said. "There is the possible presence of a new particle that is coming out of the study of a powerful neutral beam.

"It isn't the power of the neutral beam; it's this particular interaction in the Earth's atmosphere," Nagle said, in a telephone interview.

Yodh said the discovery should lead to new insights about sources of energy in the Universe and about the elementary structure of matter.

"Both of them are extremely relevant to our understanding of our Universe. I think that is the main impact it will make on society," Yodh said.

Yodh said scientists have come up with several explanations for the strange beam, which also has been detected by observatories in Arizona and Hawaii. One explanation is that it is made of a previously unknown particle.

Earth is called target of unknown particles

By Walter Sullivan
(Reprinted from The Arizona Daily Star,
March 21, 1985)

NEW YORK–Astrophysicists say they believe a cosmic power source far out in space may be bombarding the Earth with subatomic particles different from any known to science.

Recordings taken deep in a mine at Soudan, Minn., an Ohio salt mine and beneath a World War II bunker at the University of Kiel in West Germany are believed to include scores of high-energy particles from the general direction of Cygnus X-3, a double-star system in the constellation Cygnus.

Scientists said yesterday that they were at a loss to explain the new data in terms of known forms of radiation, and stressed that the recordings needed much more analysis.

But they said the data called into question the suggestion made several weeks ago, on the basis of particles detected in a salt mine beneath Lake Erie, that Cygnus X-3 may be a major source of extremely high energy neutrinos.

Neutrinos are the most penetrating and elusive of all known subatomic particles. They can pass through the Earth or almost any amount of detecting material without producing any effect.

In recent days, reports of the Minnesota and Ohio observations have prompted underground observatories elsewhere to seek verification, including those in the Frejus and Mont Blanc tunnels that link France and Italy under the Alps.

Dr. Donald Cundy of CERN, the European Organization for Nuclear Research in Geneva, Switzerland, said yesterday that his recordings under Mont Blanc had shown "something interesting," but he was not prepared to say more.

One member of the Ohio salt mine team, Dr. John Learned of the University of Hawaii, who has analyzed the observations there, says he is "pretty well convinced" that some new form of physics is involved in the observed particles.

The bunker observations in West Germany were actually reported several years ago, but until now were widely regarded as an experimental error.

Cygnus X-3 was originally identified as a source of powerful X-rays. It is now believed to be two extremely dense stars circling one another at close range and, in some unknown manner, emitting profuse, high-energy radiation in tempo with the motion of the two objects around one another every 4.8 hours.

In analyzing the salt mine data for evidence of neutrinos from Cygnus X-3, scientists assumed those that had passed through thousands of miles of rock would be most easily distinguished from other forms of radiation. The search, therefore, focused on particle tracks originating when Cygnus X-3 was below the horizon or very low in the sky.

On learning of the salt mine results, the Minnesota group began examining their data, but included arrivals from directly overhead. They found that candidate particles arrived readily when Cygnus was high in the sky but not when it was below the horizon.

This indicated that, unlike neutrinos, the particles can traverse only a limited amount of rock. Further, far too many particles were recorded for them to have the elusive character of the ghostly neutrinos.

In any case, the particles detected are assumed to be muons–heavy, short-lived counterparts of electrons–produced by high-energy particles hitting material in the detectors or nearby walls.

Mysterious gravity field tows galaxies

Los Angeles Times
Washington Post News Service
Saturday, January 13, 1990

ARLINGTON, Va.–Scientists said Thursday they have proved a mysterious gravitational field is forcing our galaxy to streak toward a distant point in the southern sky at nearly 400 miles per second.

The existence of the "Great Attractor" was first postulated in 1987 by astronomers Alan Dressler of the Carnegie Institution and Sandra Faber of the University of California, Santa Cruz, along with five colleagues who have been branded the "Seven Samurai" because of their slashing attack on conventional theory.

The controversial announcement immediately plunged the scientists into debate with many of their colleagues who doubted the Great Attractor, as Dressler named it, really existed. But they returned to the fray this week during the winter meeting of the American Astronomical Society armed with evidence that supports their original contention that a giant region of dense mass is pulling other galaxies toward it over a vast region of space.

In their recent observations Dressler and his colleagues conclude that more than a hundred galaxies are being influenced by the huge gravitational field. And other teams of scientists, including one headed by Robert A. Schommer of Rutgers University, have developed independent evidence that the Great Attractor is even greater than had been thought.

The center of Great Attractor is about 150 million light years away, the scientists reported.

A light year is the distance light travels in a year, nearly 6 trillion miles.

Despite the fact that the Great Attractor is so far away, its gravitational field is so powerful that it is tugging on galaxies that lie hundreds of millions of light years away, the scientists said.

And therein lies a mystery.

Scientists have long theorized that the universe is smooth and reasonably homogeneous, and they see no reason why it should have giant "lumps" of concentrated matter.

And there is at this point no clear understanding of just what the material is that gives the Great Attractor its enormous mass.

The discovery was "incompatible with the smoothness of the universe's background radiation," Dressler said. "Now we know we have found a very large lump," and that has sent theorists back to their computers.

Dressler and his colleagues also believe that there are probably many regions like the Great Attractor throughout the universe.

The discovery of the Great Attractor was announced in 1987 when the "Seven Samauri" had very little data to back up their claim.

The astronomers had been surveying a large segment of the sky, visible only from the Southern Hemisphere, when they discovered that some galaxies were moving at an astonishing speed toward some unseen object.

The scientists were not sure what was causing the strange

movement, and they were hampered by the fact that they were able to measure the movement of only a few nearby galaxies.

Dressler said Thursday that they were particularly concerned that they had not been able to determine if galaxies on the other side of the Great Attractor were being pulled back.

But in the last couple of years he and Faber have studied 139 additional galaxies in the region and found evidence that all are influenced by the Great Attractor.

The following is reprinted from *Parade*, "Ask Marilyn" from May, 1990

Which is the most powerful force in the universe–gravity or magnetism?

–I.J.A.
Staten Island, N.Y.

Gravity is feeble compared to magnetism. At equal distances, if we give gravitation interaction a value of 4, we'd have to give electromagnetic interaction a value of, incredibly, 10,000,000,000,000,000,000,000,000,000,000,000. (Just think–you can overcome the force of the entire earth's gravity with the little magnet that you stick on your refrigerator!)

Nature's triple whammy

By Mary Shanklin
USA TODAY
December 31, 1989

A triple celestial phenomenon that hasn't occurred in a generation may leave USA coastlines flooded in record tides next week.

"The forces of sky and sea are merging, and the effects could be devastating," said Fergus Wood, author of *Tidal Dynamics*.

On New Year's Eve:

■ Earth will be nearest the sun in its annual orbit, called perihelion.

■ The moon will be closest to Earth in its orbit, called perigee.

■ Sun, moon and Earth will be aligned.

That means a stronger-than-normal gravity pull, causing tides a foot above normal Sunday through Jan. 4, Woods said.

Possible trouble spots: Carolina coasts, Puget Sound, Bay of Maine.

Four weeks ago, the three bodies were nearly in line, causing floods on the Carolina and Southern California coasts.

In 1962, the same pattern combined with a storm to kill 40 people along the East Coast.

Astronomers are puzzled by gigantic object

By Malcolm W. Brown
1991 The New York Times
April 11, 1991

Astronomers reported Monday that they had discovered a dark, mysterious and almost inconceivably massive object lurking within a shell of luminous gas that is circulating around two colliding galaxies at speeds of almost 2 million miles an hour.

If the object is a black hole, it is 10 to 100 times as massive as any black hole previously known or even believed to be possible.

The object's enormous mass puts it in a class astronomers have never encountered before, according to the astronomers who found it.

Another possibility, the discoverers say, is that the object is a dormant quasar of the kind from which galaxies are believed to have been born more than 10 billion years ago, when the universe was young.

But the scientists acknowledge that these and several other possible explanations of the peculiar object are difficult to reconcile with established astrophysical theories.

The discovery, described in a paper that will be published tomorrow by Astrophysical Journal, was made by Dr. Joss Bland-Hawthorn of Rice University, Dr. Andrew S. Wilson of the University of Maryland and Dr. R. Brent Tully of the University of Hawaii, using the 88-inch telescope atop the Mauna Kea volcano in Hawaii.

The group found the object while studying a bright galaxy named NGC 6240, which lies 300 million light-years from Earth.

The dark object within NGC 6240 has not been observed directly. But the direction and velocity of gases surrounding it are affected by the object, and the motions of these gases cause shifts in the spectrum of light they send toward Earth.

The group says that NGC 6240 consists of two whirling disks of matter, which may be galaxies in collision.

In one disk, the rotation patterns of gases is characteristic of all common galaxies, but in the other the gases are rotating in patterns and at speeds that can be explained only by assuming that they are orbiting an extremely massive object.

This object must be 100 billion times as massive as the Sun–about the same mass as Earth's galaxy, the Milky Way–but occupying a space no more than one ten-thousandth as great.

Bland-Hawthorn said the object might be a supermassive black hole. But if it is, he added, it would be 100 million to a billion times as massive as the largest black hole astronomers believe to exist.

A black hole absorbs all light or other radiation reaching it, and emits none of its own by which a distant observer could see it.

But disks of matter scavenged from interstellar space are drawn toward black holes, and as matter spirals inward, it is heated to such temperatures that it emits X-rays and gamma rays.

The discoverers of the mysterious object plan to use the Rosat satellite to check NGC 6240 for X-ray emissions, and they hope to use the Gamma Ray Observatory, which was launched Sunday by the space shuttle Atlantis to look for black hole gamma radiation.

The detection of either X-rays or gamma rays would support the view that the object is a black hole.

"We're not certain at this point whether we're seeing one galaxy tearing another galaxy apart, or whether one galaxy is being disrupted by this supermassive object at the center of the other galaxy," Bland-Hawthorn said.

Mystery blob brightest object ever found

By Nicholas Moore
Reuters
(The Phoenix Gazette
Thursday, June 27, 1991)

LONDON–Astronomers claim to have spotted the brightest object ever discovered in the universe.

But it appears so faint when seen from the Earth, being so remote in space and time, that they almost missed it. And they don't know what it is, either.

The 13 astronomers from the United States and Britain reported to the scientific journal *Nature* that they had called the mysterious blob IRAS Faint Source 10214 + 4724.

They found it by accident on the 40th and last night of a trawl through the heavens looking for something else through a telescope in the Canary Islands.

It emits "enormous" luminosity, radiating 30,000 times the energy of the Milky Way, if calculations are right.

Nature said it may be "a quasar cocooned in a dusty galaxy."

Some quasars (stars like heavenly objects) are galaxies with black holes devouring matter in the middle of them. But *Nature* said this discovery could be "a protogalaxy–a massive galaxy in the process of formation."

Scientists have been hunting for a youthful galaxy for decades in the hope of learning more about how the universe evolved.

A British astronomer, Patrick Moore, explained that "they were doing a survey of quasars. When you're trawling for quasars, you are bound to find them, and this was one that came up in the net."

He said the distance of the object was about 12 billion light years so that light from it "began its journey long before the sun or the Earth existed."

"We are seeing this thing as it was when it was very young. We are looking back into the very early history of the universe at how we all evolved. But just how it started is something we don't know."

Experts surprised as satellite finds gamma-ray bursts throughout sky

(Reprinted from Star Ledger, *Newark, NJ*
September 26, 1991)

WASHINGTON (AP)–An astronomy satellite has detected short, powerful bursts of gamma rays in virtually every corner of the sky, suggesting the signals may originate from sources near the edge of the universe, scientists said yesterday.

Gerald Fishman of the Marshall Space Flight Center said an instrument called the Burst and Transient Source Experiment aboard NASA's Gamma Ray Observatory has detected 117 gamma ray bursts since the satellite was launched April 7.

"They are randomly scattered throughout the sky," Fishman said at a news conference yesterday. He said the scattered sources came as a surprise because it was believed that gamma ray bursts detected by earlier instruments were all coming from the center of the Milky Way Galaxy and were thought to be relatively rare.

Instead, said Fishman, the bursts are occurring about once a day and are coming from every point in the sky.

"Gamma-ray bursts have been observed for 25 years, but the source of these bright flashes in the sky remains a mystery," said Neil Gehrels, the NASA project scientist for the Gamma Ray Observatory. "Determining the sources and their positions in the sky is one of the Holy Grails of astrophysics."

Gamma rays are an invisible, high energy form of radiation. The gamma ray signals are thought to be produced from such events and objects as solar flares, black holes, quasars and supernovae. NASA's Gamma Ray Observatory is a 17-ton satellite.

Before the satellite's launch, Gehrels said that gamma ray bursts were thought to come from neutron stars and would be seen to come from the center of the Milky Way galaxy.

Since the bursts are randomly distributed, the scientist said that the source must be either small, exotic objects very near the solar system, or from "monstrously powerful distant objects." The sources could be in very distant corners of the universe, he said.

"If they are beyond our galaxy, then the energy released in the brief one-second flash of gamma rays is many times the total energy released when a star explodes as a supernova," said Gehrels.

Fishman said there is no optical counterpart to the bursts. This means that astronomers have not found stars that radiate in visible light that would explain the sources of the bursts.

NASA also announced that the name of the Gamma Ray Observatory was being changed to the Arthur Holly Compton Gamma Ray Observatory. Compton, an American physicist who died in 1962, conducted a series of experiments on cosmic rays in the 1930s and played a key role in early work on gamma rays.

AVAILABLE TAPES
YOUR TIME IS AT HAND
by
Patricia Diane Cota-Robles

A series has been produced by Patricia to coincide with the chapters in this book. The tapes will assist each person to absorb the maximum benefit from this Sacred Knowledge.

CHAPTER ONE...SET OF THREE TAPES
   YOU HAVE COME TO SAVE THE EARTH...
   AND YOUR TIME IS AT HAND
   PART I – PART II – PART III $27.00
                                * + P & H $ 2.00

CHAPTER TWO...SET OF TWO TAPES
   NOW IS THE OPPORTUNITY FOR LIMITLESS
   PHYSICAL PERFECTION
   PART I – PART II $18.00
                                  * + P & H $ 2.00

CHAPTER FOUR...ONE TAPE
   THE GIFT TO RECLAIM YOUR PROSPERITY $ 9.00
                                  * + P & H $ 2.00

BOOK – YOUR TIME IS AT HAND $16.00
                                * + P & H $ 2.00
                                  (for first book)
                                   $ .75
                           (for each additional book)

*POSTAGE & HANDLING
Add $4.50 for Canada & Mexico
Add $8.00 for all other countries

BOOKS & TAPES SUBTOTAL _____

+ POSTAGE & HANDLING _____

TOTAL _____

(continued on other side)

NAME _____

ADDRESS _____

CITY _____ STATE _____ ZIP _____

COUNTRY _____ TELEPHONE _____

Please send check or money order for entire order to:
The New Age Study of Humanity's Purpose, Inc.
P.O. Box 41883, Tucson, Arizona 85717   U.S.A.
FAX # (602) 323-8252

WHEN PAYING BY VISA OR MASTERCARD,
PLEASE FILL OUT AND RETURN THIS COUPON.

VISA   ☐   MASTERCARD   ☐

Amount to be charged _____

Account Number _____

Card Expires _____

PRINT Name on Card _____

Signature _____

ADDITIONAL BOOKS & AVAILABLE TAPES

TAKE CHARGE OF YOUR LIFE
by Patricia Diane Cota-Robles

Take Charge of Your Life

Patricia Diane Cota-Robles

$8.95   162 Pages

There is an awakening taking place on this Planet, an increased awareness that is prompting people to search for solutions to the trials and tribulations of their daily lives.

Take Charge Of Your Life is elegant in its simplicity, clearly presented, and easy to understand. It is a unique and important book which presents concrete, practical step-by-step instructions that will give you specific tools and techniques necessary to ATTAIN YOUR FINANCIAL FREEDOM; CREATE WONDERFUL, LOVING RELATIONSHIPS; REACH YOUR OPTIMUM LEVEL OF SUCCESS AND EXCELLENCE: RESTORE YOUR BODY TO VIBRANT HEALTH: DEVELOP YOUR HIGHEST SPIRITUAL POTENTIAL; and TRULY BECOME THE MASTER OF YOUR LIFE *instead of the victim of your experiences.*

A series of tapes has been produced by Patricia Diane Cota-Robles to coincide with the book *TAKE CHARGE OF YOUR LIFE.* The tapes consist of a lesson, guided visualizations and meditations to help us utilize the tools presented in the book easily and effectively.

AVAILABLE TAPES FOR...
TAKE CHARGE OF YOUR LIFE
by
Patricia Diane Cota-Robles

A series of tapes has also been produced by Patricia Diane Cota-Robles to coincide with the book *TAKE CHARGE OF YOUR LIFE.* The tapes consist of a lesson, guided visualizations and meditations to help us utilize the tools presented in the book easily and effectively.

1. **YOU CAN TAKE CHARGE OF YOUR LIFE** $9.00
   The Key to Self-Mastery Is Self-Awareness–The Power of Thought–Monitoring Your Emotions–Creative Visualizations–Setting Goals

2. **UNCONDITIONAL LOVE** $9.00
   Transforming Your Relationships–The Power of Unconditional Love–Four Steps to Love Your Negative Energy FREE

3. **THE KEY TO FINANCIAL FREEDOM** $9.00
   Poverty Is NOT A Virtue–Clearing Your Relationships With Money–Money Is A Source of Energy...PERIOD–Opening Up to God's Limitless Flow of Abundance

4. **HEALING** $9.00
   Maintaining Health In Your Physical Bodies–Disease Is Often Self-Inflicted–Mental Aspects of Dis-ease and Healing–Visualization for Healing–Breathing Exercises

5. **MAGNETIZING PERFECTION INTO YOUR LIFE THROUGH THE CHAKRA CENTERS** $9.00
   Demystifying the Chakras–Chakras, Your Body's Electrical System–Cleansing and Balancing the Chakras–Using the Chakras As An Effective Tool to Harmonize Your Life

6. **HARMONY, COLOR AND MUSIC** $9.00
   The Use of Color and Music to Help You Reach Your Highest Potential–Color and Qualities of the Seven Spiritual Rays–Color Meditations–Music, A Sacred Science

7. **ALIGNING WITH YOUR DIVINE PURPOSE FOR "THE CAMPAIGN OF THE EARTH"** $9.00
   Recognizing Our True God Reality–Eliminating Low Self-Esteem–Fulfilling Our Mission On Earth

8. **MEDITATIONS TO TRANSFORM YOUR LIFE** $9.00
   Guided Meditations, Visualizations and Affirmations to Help You Establish Positive Thinking Patterns and Transmute Old Belief Systems That No Longer Support Your Highest Good

9. **GETTING IN TOUCH WITH YOUR
HIGHER SELF** **$9.00**
Communing With the God Presence Within–The Key to Spiritual
Freedom–Entering the Realms of Illumined Truth–Perceiving Your
Divine Plan

10. **THE WORLD HEALING MEDITATION
AND PLANETARY TRANSFORMATION** **$9.00**
Balancing and Purifying Your Four Lower Bodies–Become the
Clearest, Most Powerful Channel of Light You Can Possibly Be–Trans-
forming the Earth Into FREEDOM'S HOLY STAR–Healing Planet
Earth

The tapes in the *TAKE CHARGE OF YOUR LIFE* series
are $9.00 each plus $1.50 postage and handling for each tape,
or you may purchase the entire set of 10 tapes at a SPECIAL
DISCOUNT RATE OF $75.00 plus $5.50 postage and handling–**A SAVINGS OF $15.00.**

To order see enclosed order form.

ORDER FORM
THE NEW AGE STUDY OF HUMANITY'S PURPOSE

Number of Copies

TAKE CHARGE OF YOUR LIFE
         BOOK $8.95 + $2.00 P & H _____

TAKE CHARGE OF YOUR LIFE...TAPES

1. **YOU CAN TAKE CHARGE OF YOUR LIFE**
   $9.00 + 1.50 P&H   _____

2. **UNCONDITIONAL LOVE**
   TRANSFORMATION
   $9.00 + $1.50 P & H   _____

3. **THE KEY TO FINANCIAL FREEDOM**
   $9.00 + $1.50 P & H   _____

4. **HEALING $9.00 + $1.50 P & H**   _____

5. **MAGNETIZING PERFECTION INTO**
   YOUR LIFE THROUGH THE CHAKRA
   CENTERS $9.00 + $1.50 P & H   _____

6. **HARMONY, COLOR AND MUSIC**
   $9.00 + $1.50 P & H   _____

7. **ALIGNING WITH YOUR DIVINE**
   PURPOSE FOR "THE CAMPAIGN
   FOR THE EARTH"
   $9.00 + $1.50 P & H   _____

8. **MEDITATIONS TO TRANSFORM**
   YOUR LIFE $9.00 + $1.50 P & H   _____

9. **GETTING IN TOUCH WITH YOUR**
   HIGHER SELF $9.00 + $1.50 P & H   _____

10. **WORLD HEALING MEDITATION–**
    PLANETARY TRANSFORMATION
    $9.00 + $1.50 P & H   _____

11. **ENTIRE SET OF TAPES**
    $75.00 + $5.50 P & H *(SAVE $15.00)* _____

                    BOOKS & TAPES SUBTOTAL _____
                    + POSTAGE & HANDLING _____
                                    TOTAL _____

(continued on other side)

NAME _____

ADDRESS _____

CITY _____ STATE _____ ZIP _____

COUNTRY _____ TELEPHONE _____

Please send check or money order for entire order to:
The New Age Study of Humanity's Purpose, Inc.
P.O. Box 41883, Tucson, Arizona 85717   U.S.A.
FAX # (602) 323-8252

WHEN PAYING BY VISA OR MASTERCARD,
PLEASE FILL OUT AND RETURN THIS COUPON.

VISA ☐   MASTERCARD ☐

Amount to be charged _____

Account Number _____

Card Expires _____

PRINT Name on Card _____

Signature _____

THE NEXT STEP...
Re-unification with the Presence of God within Our Hearts

by
Patricia Diane Cota-Robles

$14.98   369 Pages

Now, during this critical moment on Earth, we are being given unparalleled knowledge and wisdom that will enable each of us to re-unite with the part of our consciousness that ALWAYS aspires to the highest level of EXCELLENCE.

As the vibratory rate of the Planet increases, we are being lifted up closer to the realms of Illumined Truth in the Octaves of Perfection. This Realm pulsates with the knowledge and wisdom of the Ages. As this Illumination enters our consciousness, it provides us with very practical tangible tools and techniques that open the door for us to go within and tap the Power of our Divinity. When this occurs, our true God-Self bursts the bonds of human limitation and takes full dominion of our Lives.

Once we have re-united with our Higher Self–our God Presence "I AM"–It will guide us unerringly, as we create for ourselves Lives of JOY, HAPPINESS, ABUNDANCE, HEALTH, LOVE, FULFILLMENT, PURPOSE, SUCCESS and VICTORY.

This very timely book contains within its pages the Sacred Knowledge pouring forth from the Realms of TRUTH. As we apply this knowledge in our everyday Lives, we will experience a Transformation taking place. Our Lives will change. They will begin to reflect the Happiness, Harmony and Success we have been longing for. As we develop the simple skills taught in this significant book, we will experience more Loving relationships, Financial Freedom, Vibrant Health, Happiness, Fulfilling Careers, Spiritual Growth, Joyous Selfless Service, Inner Peace, Optimism and TOTAL SELF-MASTERY.

"Know the TRUTH and the TRUTH shall set you FREE!"

The Next Step...
Re-unification with the Presence of God within our Hearts
Patricia Diane Cota-Robles

Patricia Diane Cota-Robles has also produced a series of tapes that coincide with the chapters of the book. The tapes will assist each person to absorb the maximum benefit from this Sacred Knowledge.

Each tape contains important information exercises, visualizations, affirmations, meditations and techniques that will set us FREE from our self-inflicted lack and limitation.

SPECIAL DISCOUNT–SAVE $25.00
by ordering the entire set of tapes.
$120.00 for all 16 tapes

THE NEXT STEP...
A. GOD'S WILL **$9.00**
The Will of God Is Perfection–Humanity's Fall From the Will of God–Exposing the World of Illusion in the Light of Reality–Humanity's Return Journey Back to the Will of God–Effectively Utilizing God's Will in Our Daily Lives.

B. THE WORLD HEALING MEDITATION AND PLANETARY TRANSFORMATION **$9.00**
This meditation tape cleanses our four lower bodies and prepares us to be the clearest possible channels of Healing Light–Visualization for the Transformation of Planet Earth into Freedom's Holy Star.

C. ENLIGHTENMENT **$9.00**
"Ye Are Gods"–In The Beginning..."I AM"–The Original Divine Plan–Earth's Return Journey Home

D. DIVINE LOVE **$9.00**
The Power of Divine Love–Love...And Let It Begin With Me–The Children of Love: Tolerance, Patience, Kindness, Humanitarianism, Reverence, Balance–Communication; The Key to Harmonious Relationships

E. PURITY **$9.00**
Purity is the Heart of Creation–The Miracle of Resurrection–Resurrecting The Divine Pattern Within–The Immaculate Concept–The Goal of Life Is the Ascension

F. TRUTH **$9.00**
The Empowerment of All God Qualities on Earth through the Supreme Initiation.

G. MINISTERING GRACE **$9.00**
Ministration is an activity of Grace–The Fourth Dimension is Established On Earth–The Opening of the Seventh and Final Angelic Vortex–Accepting the Power Within: Becoming the Divine Image Embodied in Flesh.

H. STAR∗LINK 88 . . . . **$9.00**
This is a Powerful Activity of Light in which Humanity unites with the Angelic Kingdom to Assist this Sweet Earth as She Ascends into the Realms of Harmony and Balance.

**I. TRANSMUTING THE PAST THROUGH
    THE POWER OF FORGIVENESS** **$9.00**
Utilizing the Power of Transmutation–The Violet Flame of Forgiveness and Freedom.

J. FREEDOM **$9.00**
Seven Steps to Precipitation: The Science of Succeeding in Your Purpose–Violet Flame Class

K. CLARITY **$9.00**
The Rebirth of our Planetary Identity into our God Identity–Through the Ray of Clarity, the Traps of the World of Illusion are Revealed

L. HARMONY **$9.00**
Harmony and Balance: The Path to our Eternal Freedom–The Twelve Universal Laws

M. ETERNAL PEACE **$9.00**
The Great Silence–Eternal Peace, The Open Door to Spiritual Freedom and Liberty

N. DIVINE PURPOSE **$9.00**
Happiness and Joy: Our Divine Birthright, Our Choice–Fulfilling Our Divine Purpose: A Step-By-Step Process

O. TRANSFORMATION **$9.00**
Transformation–Preparing for the Earth's Ascension into the Fourth Dimension

P. FROM HERE TO FOREVER **$11.00**
This tape contains wonderful songs sung by Peaches. Songs that lift the Soul and inspire the Consciousness

The tapes are $9.00 each (Peaches' tape is $11.00). plus $1.50 postage and handling per tape, or you may purchase THE ENTIRE SET OF 16 TAPES FOR A SPECIAL DISCOUNT RATE OF $120.00–**A SAVINGS OF $25.00**. Postage and handling for the complete tape package is $5.50.
To order see order form.

**The New Age Study of Humanity's Purpose
P.O. Box 41883
Tucson, Arizona 85717
FAX # (602) 323-8252**

ORDER FORM
THE NEW AGE STUDY OF HUMANITY'S PURPOSE

Number of Copies

THE NEXT STEP–BOOK
$14.98 + $2.00 P & H _____

THE NEXT STEP...TAPES

A. GOD'S WILL $9.00 + 1.50 P&H _____

B. WORLD HEALING & PLANETARY
TRANSFORMATION
$9.00 + $1.50 P & H _____

C. ENLIGHTENMENT
$9.00 + $1.50 P & H _____

D. DIVINE LOVE $9.00 + $1.50 P & H _____

E. PURITY $9.00 + $1.50 P & H _____

F. TRUTH $9.00 + $1.50 P & H _____

G. MINISTERING GRACE
$9.00 + $1.50 P & H _____

H. STAR*LINK 88 $9.00 + $1.50 P & H _____

I. TRANSMUTING THE PAST
$9.00 + $1.50 P & H _____

J. FREEDOM $9.00 + $1.50 P & H _____

K. CLARITY $9.00 + $1.50 P & H _____

L. HARMONY $9.00 + $1.50 P & H _____

M. ETERNAL PEACE
$9.00 + $1.50 P &H _____

N. DIVINE PURPOSE
$9.00 + $1.50 P & H _____

O. TRANSFORMATION
$9.00 + $1.50 P & H _____

P. FROM HERE TO FOREVER
$11.00 + $1.50 P & H _____

Q. ENTIRE SET OF TAPES
$120.00 + $5.50 P & H *(SAVE $25.00)* _____

SUBTOTAL BOOKS & TAPES _____

+ POSTAGE & HANDLING _____

TOTAL _____

(continued on other side)

NAME _____

ADDRESS _____

CITY _____ STATE _____ ZIP _____

COUNTRY _____ TELEPHONE _____

Please send check or money order for entire order to:
The New Age Study of Humanity's Purpose, Inc.
P.O. Box 41883, Tucson, Arizona 85717   U.S.A.
FAX # (602) 323-8252

WHEN PAYING BY VISA OR MASTERCARD, PLEASE FILL OUT AND RETURN THIS COUPON.

VISA ☐   MASTERCARD ☐

Amount to be charged _____

Account Number _____

Card Expires _____

PRINT Name on Card _____

Signature _____

ADDITIONAL BOOK & AVAILABLE TAPES

THE AWAKENING...
Eternal Youth, Vibrant Health, Radiant Beauty

by
Patricia Diane Cota-Robles

194 Pages $12.95

Aging, disease, deterioration and death as we know it were never part of the original Divine Plan on Earth. These miserable maladies are part of our human miscreation. They are the result of the "fall of man," a tragic time aeons ago when Humanity began experimenting with our creative faculties of thought and feeling in ways that were conflicting with God's Will. These distortions of our physical body have become such a common part of our everyday reality that we have accepted them as "normal." Actually nothing could be more abnormal.

Now, as we lift up in consciousness and tap the Realms of Illumined Truth, we are awakening within us the Truth of who we really are...Sons and Daughters of God, and we are realizing that the Divine Plan for Planet Earth and all Her life is Limitless Physical Perfection. This is not some far fetched dream, this is a very real opportunity.

Contained within the pages of this important, timely book is the Sacred Knowledge from the Realms of Truth that will enable each of us to Transform our bodies into ETERNAL YOUTH, VIBRANT HEALTH and RADIANT BEAUTY.

There is a set of tapes that coincides with this book that will assist you in assimilating this Truth. See order form on the back of this page.

ORDER FORM
THE NEW AGE STUDY OF HUMANITY'S PURPOSE

THE AWAKENING...
ETERNAL YOUTH, VIBRANT HEALTH, RADIANT BEAUTY

Book $12.95 + $2.00 P&H*   _____
(for first book)
for each additional book $.75 P&H

THE AWAKENING...TAPES

1. THE TRANSFIGURATION OF OUR PHYSICAL BODY
   $9.00 + $1.50 P&H   _____

2. BECOMING YOUR HOLY CHRIST SELF
   THE TRUE MEANING OF "THE SECOND COMING"
   PART I & II (2 Tapes) $18.00 + $2.00 P&H   _____

3. MORNING EXERCISES FOR PHYSICAL
   TRANSFORMATION AND
   EVENING EXERCISES FOR PHYSICAL TRANSFORMATION
   (2 Tapes) $18.00 + $2.00 P&H   _____

4. OWNER'S MANUAL FOR THE PHYSICAL BODY
   ATTAINING ETERNAL YOUTH, VIBRANT HEALTH,
   RADIANT BEAUTY $9.00 + $1.50 P&H   _____

*Postage & Handling
Add $4.50 for Canada & Mexico
Add $8.00 for all other countries

BOOKS & TAPES SUBTOTAL _____
+ POSTAGE & HANDLING _____
TOTAL _____

Name _____

Address _____

City _____ State _____ Zip _____

Country _____ Telephone _____

Please send check or money order to The New Age Study of Humanity's Purpose, Inc.,
P.O. Box 41883, Tucson, AZ 85717 U.S.A. FAX # (602) 323-8252

WHEN PAYING BY VISA OR MASTER CARD, PLEASE FILL OUT AND RETURN THIS COUPON
VISA ☐   MASTERCARD ☐

Amt. to be charged _____ Expiration on Card _____

Account Number _____

PRINT Name on Card _____

Signature _____

INFORMATION ABOUT VISIONARY ART

During this very special time of Planetary Transformation, wonderful tools are being given to Humanity which will help us align with the higher realms of Perfection enabling us to Heal ourselves and this Sweet Earth.

In this time of awakening, Art has expanded into a much higher octave of service. It is no longer being used just for aesthetic appreciation, but now it is being used as a vehicle to reveal to Humanity the perfection of Heaven. We are truly multi-dimensional Beings, and, as we gaze upon the visionary art of awakened artists, we will activate within ourselves the memory of our own Divinity and our connection with the Realms of Truth.

The Light of God is pouring into the Earth as never before, and we are receiving unprecedented assistance from the entire Company of Heaven. When visions of the Divine Intervention occurring now on Earth are available to us, we can energize the activities more easily and greatly enhance their effectiveness.

Each print of visionary art contains within it the energy, vibration and consciousness of the image shown. When we place the visionary art in our homes and workplaces, the Light of the Divine Vision portrayed in the image begins to resonate through our environment, lifting us and blessing all who enter our sphere of influence.

Sharon Nichols' art reflects many dimensions of Healing that are simultaneously occurring on Earth at this time. We have displayed the art in three different categories. Each category has a different frequency and vibration designed to fulfill a particular facet of the plan of Transformation.

As you look upon each visionary print, bring it into your Heart Flame and ask the Presence of God blazing in your Heart to reveal to you which prints will help you fulfill your Divine Mission on Earth most powerfully. Listen for your inner voice. Observe which prints seem to pull on your Heartstrings. Then, respond to your Heart's call, according to your highest good.

For full color brochure write to:
> The New Age Study of Humanity's Purpose
> P.O. Box 41883
> Tucson, Arizona 85717
> FAX (602) 323-8252